Making Sense of the Cross

Leader Guide

AUGSBURG FORTRESS
Minneapolis

MAKING SENSE OF THE CROSS Leader Guide

This Leader Guide is intended for use along with the book *Making Sense of the Cross* (978-0-8066-9851-9). Session introductions by author David Lose are also available on DVD (978-0-8066-9853-3). These resources are also available for purchase online at www.augsburgfortress.org.

Copyright © 2011 Augsburg Fortress. All rights reserved. Except for brief quotations in critical articles or reviews, no part of this book may be reproduced in any manner without prior written permission from the publisher. For more information, visit: www.augsburgfortress.org/copyrights or write to: Permissions, Augsburg Fortress, Box 1209, Minneapolis, MN 55440-1209.

Scripture quotations, unless otherwise marked, are from New Revised Standard Version Bible, © copyright 1989 Division of Christian Education of the National Council of Churches of Christ in the United States of America. Used by permission. All rights reserved.

ISBN: 978-0-8066-9852-6

Writer: David J. Lose
Editors: Laurie J. Hanson and Scott Tunseth

Cover design: Joe Vaughan
Interior design: Ivy Palmer Skrade
Typesetting: Tory Herman

The paper used in this publication meets the minimum requirements of American National Standard for Information Sciences—Permanence of Paper for Printed Library Materials, ANSI Z329.48-1984

Manufactured in the U.S.A.

15 14 13 12 11 1 2 3 4 5 6 7 8 9 10

Contents

1	INTRODUCTION
1	*Welcome*
2	*Guiding Convictions*
4	*Overview of the Leader Guide and Session Components*
6	*Advice and Counsel*
8	*Session Schedules and Variations*
9	*Using a Retreat Format*
10	*Covenant*
11	*Invitation Letter*
12	SESSION 1: A MAN HANGING ON A TREE
19	SESSION 2: PORTRAITS AND PERSPECTIVES
27	SESSION 3: RANSOM AND VICTORY
34	SESSION 4: SUBSTITUTION, SATISFACTION, AND SACRIFICE
41	SESSION 5: EXAMPLE AND ENCOURAGEMENT
48	SESSION 6: EVENT AND EXPERIENCE

Introduction

Welcome

from David Lose, author of *Making Sense of the Cross*

I am both pleased and grateful that you've offered your time and energy to serve as a leader for this study. The role you will play in helping others to better understand the nature and importance of Jesus' cross and resurrection is so important. I know that it takes both effort and commitment to lead a class like this effectively, and I appreciate that you've offered to do that.

To help you in the role you've accepted, this Introduction to the Leader Guide will do three things:
- share several guiding convictions of the course,
- go over the pattern of the Leader Guide and review each component of the sessions, and
- offer some advice ahead of time on how to lead this study most effectively.

A further word before jumping in: Sometimes when we are invited into leadership roles, we wonder if we are adequately prepared. I want to assure you from the outset that the primary requirements for leading this course are a curious and open mind, a desire to welcome others into a conversation about the cross, and a willingness to learn from the other participants in the class. You do not need to be an expert in Christian theology or the Bible to lead this course, and you should never feel that you need to have answers to all the questions others may raise. You are as much a learner as the other participants. In fact, you may very well find you learn even more because of your additional preparation; I regularly find I never learn a subject so well as when I prepare to teach it.

I hope and expect that leading these sessions will be a rewarding experience for you. I know already that others will benefit from your effort. Please accept my thanks in advance for this.

Guiding Convictions

Two convictions I have about the nature of conversations and the importance of questions shape both the content and the structure of *Making Sense of the Cross* and this study course. A third conviction about the nature of biblical faith will be helpful to consider as well.

1. Conversations

Countless experiences have taught me that there are few, if any, ways better at helping one learn something than by talking about it. From study sessions in college to long and memorable all-night conversations with friends, there's just something about hashing out an issue with others that makes a subject easier to understand, talk about, and use. Maybe it's that you have to put your knowledge to work in a conversation, fashioning an argument or thinking through how you might clearly explain what you mean. Or maybe it's the lively, often unpredictable twists and turns that are part and parcel of conversing with a real, live person that make conversations such important vehicles for learning. Whatever it is, I just know that in, with, and through conversations with others, I've probably learned more than from all the books I've ever read or lectures I've heard.

This conviction shapes *Making Sense of the Cross* in two important ways. First, the book is written as a conversation. This may feel a little awkward at first, as we're used to reading prose in one voice and point of view, but many have commented that they enjoy "listening in" to this kind of conversation and that, indeed, they find themselves participating right alongside the two voices in the narrative. Second, and just as important, this leader guide proposes a class design that has conversation at its heart. Again and again, people will be invited to engage in conversation with each other—thinking, talking, listening, responding—all with the conviction that we have a tremendous amount to teach each other and that the best way to share, teach, and learn is through conversation.

2. Questions

Somewhere along the way, many of us picked up the idea that because questions supposedly betray ignorance, they are something we should avoid. That is, we fear that others will unconsciously equate the number of questions we ask with our intellectual inadequacy. Sometimes we do indeed ask questions because we don't know something, and in those cases I can't think of a better way of learning. (Isn't it, after all, the truly foolish person who never asks a question for fear of looking foolish?) And so questions become an important vehicle for learning.

At other times, questions are a mark of just how much we already understand. Think about it: how could we begin to ask a particular question about Einstein's theory of relativity if we hadn't already mastered many of the basics? In fact, only someone who knows a lot more about physics than I do can even ask a coherent question about relativity. Questions, then, far from betraying a lack of intelligence, are actually the mark of a lively, sharp, and curious mind.

Similarly, there is a persistent notion among some Christians that doubt is the opposite of faith. Even a relatively cursory reading of Scripture, however, provides ample evidence that doubt is an integral part of the life of faith. Almost everyone in the Bible doubts God's promises at one time or another, and that includes not only the disciples but even Jesus, and so we should feel free to trust that God works through our doubts, not in spite of them.

Recognizing that questions and doubt are part of a robust biblical faith means that we will put a high value on the questions we have about faith, about life, and even about God. Therefore this book is, again, regularly moved forward by the questions and, at times, doubts of the conversation partners. Similarly, it will be essential to help people in this study to come to believe that there are no "dumb questions" by creating a safe and welcoming environment where people feel comfortable sharing both their faith and their doubts and can voice both their insights and their questions.

In fact, the issue of "Insights and Questions" probably deserves another moment of reflection. Most of us are familiar with the IQ, or Intelligence Quotient, test. By and large, we think of an IQ test as a measure of intelligence according to what *we already know*. In much of life, however, and certainly for the purposes of this course, we will instead think of IQ as a measure of intelligence according to what *we are presently learning and still curious about*. For this reason, at the beginning and end of each session, we will take a few moments to dwell on the Insights and Questions (IQ) we have about the material at hand. The more comfortable we are in sharing what we are learning and questioning, the more enjoyable and profitable will be our time together.

3. Biblical Faith
I believe that the Bible is best understood as a collection of all kinds of different confessions of faith. These confessions take many different shapes and sizes. Some are stories while others are songs; some are legal codes and others genealogies; some are instructions for rituals, while others are romantic poetry. And some, as we will soon find out, are lengthy passion narratives. What binds all these varied confessions together is that all of them were offered by persons so gripped by an experience of God that they had to tell others. Together, these confessions of faith tell the story of God and God's people. As anyone who opens a Bible soon discovers, however, it is not the same kind of story as one you find in a novel—with a neat beginning, middle, and end. Rather, it is more like the story that emerges from a family scrapbook, filled with bits and pieces of a family's history over the generations.

Theology, at its best, helps us to make sense of the many rich and varied stories and confessions of faith in the Bible by pulling important themes from these confessions to help us see a larger story among all the many various and sundry stories in the Bible. In a sense, if we can imagine the biblical witness and our life of faith as a journey, theological doctrines are the major road markers, or signs, pointing us in the right way. That means that we think about and believe theology not because we have to—as if getting the right terms or historical background matters—but instead because theology is actually helpful to us. When theology is primarily about "believing the right things," in fact, it quickly becomes dry and dusty, but when theology helps us make sense of Scripture and our lives, it's remarkably helpful.

This is particularly true when we talk about the cross. There are a lot of strong views about the nature, purpose, and effect of the cross, and some Christians have actually made certain propositions about the cross the litmus test for measuring "true" faith. Given the complexity of the biblical witness about the cross, I think this is both unnecessary and unwise. Therefore, I think it will be very helpful to invite people to risk their views, their hunches, and their convictions about what is accomplished in the cross and resurrection of Jesus, even if they don't always agree with each other. The point isn't to understand the cross once and forever, and certainly not to be able to prove our orthodoxy over others. Rather, the goal for this study and the conversation it engenders is to have a fresh and ongoing understanding and experience of the life-transforming love of God that is poured out for us and all the world in and through Jesus' cross and resurrection.

For this reason, don't be afraid of hard questions; instead, honor both the questions and the insights people bring and trust that God can work through all of them to draw us more deeply into relationship with God and each other. Sometimes honoring questions can seem frustrating—and some in the group may want to know what the "right" answer is—but I've found that by living with the questions rather than rushing to answer them, we end up with a livelier and deeper relationship with the God we come to know most clearly in the man hanging on a tree.

Overview of the Leader Guide and Session Components

In this section, we will walk through the structure of the Leader Guide and discuss each component that makes up a session.

PREPARE

The Prepare section is designed to help you get ready for each session. Here you will find the following elements:

- *Focus Statement*—Summarizes the key learning point of the session. This can serve as a compass point to keep you oriented toward the main idea of the chapter and session.

- *Chapter Overview*—Recaps the chapter from *Making Sense of the Cross* that the session will explore. This is for your review. You may, however, use this as a starting point to outline the key concepts for participants, particularly if you decide not to use the accompanying DVD introduction to the session.

- *Before You Begin*—Offers some questions for you to think about as you prepare to meet with participants.

- *Session Instructions*—Provides a list of key things to keep in mind as you prepare to lead the session.

- *Facilitator's Prayer*—Presents a way to center yourself and prepare for the role you will play. It is the same each week, and you are encouraged to take confidence from its familiarity as well as adapt it to your needs.

Throughout the session, you will also find Teaching Tips and Supplies in the sidebar. Take time to look at these items as you prepare to lead. They provide helpful hints and additional ways to approach the session time.

GATHER

The Gather time includes three essential elements:

- *Welcome and Check-In*—Focuses on building relationships and trust so the community feels comfortable asking and addressing challenging questions. We do not learn well unless other, more basic, needs are met. One of the most basic needs participants will have is to feel welcome, accepted and safe. By spending a few moments each week to check-in, you will greatly strengthen the level of trust participants have for each other.

- **Opening Prayer**—Offers each participant the chance to be still and centered as they become open to God's Word. Each session has a different prayer written with the subject material of that session in mind. Feel free to read it aloud or adapt it. You might also use this time to invite participants to share prayer requests or offer prayers.

- **Insights and Questions (IQ) Time**—Gives participants a chance to articulate, and therefore "own," what they are learning (which is why this is one of the most important parts of the session). This time also helps participants focus their questions. Participants may be surprised by how powerful it is to name the new insights they have achieved and to listen to and learn from the insights of others. Sometimes participants will be able to answer each other's questions—adding to their confidence in discussing matters of faith. Sometimes their questions will serve to focus the conversation ahead. Either way, collecting these insights and questions upfront will be a helpful habit to develop. At the end of each session, participants will revisit their IQs in light of the discussion and study they've just experienced.

JOIN THE CONVERSATION

In this section participants will engage the central concepts and ideas of the chapter they've read in three ways.

- **Video Introduction**—Provides a summary of the chapter and an overview of the exercises and Bible study to come. If you choose not to show this, you will probably want to summarize the chapter concepts, drawing from the Chapter Overview (in the Prepare section).

- **Conversation Starters**—Focuses on two quotations directly from *Making Sense of the Cross* that capture the main ideas of each chapter. These quotations are followed by several questions designed to elicit initial conversation about the topic at hand.

- **Activity**—Gives participants a chance to put the concepts into practice, usually while working together in small groups. Here, some of the conceptual learning takes a deeper, more experiential "hold" of the participants. Many sessions also offer a Bonus Activity that can be used in addition to or instead of the main activity, depending upon your group's needs and the amount of time you have for the class session.

OPEN SCRIPTURE

Having "practiced" the concepts of the chapter during the Activity, this section engages participants in exploring Bible texts to support the key concepts of the session.

- **Bible Text**—Engages participants in Scripture using the new ideas and tools they developed during Join the Conversation. Through discussion and activities, participants deepen their understanding not only of a biblical passage, but also of the main idea or skill covered in the chapter. Most sessions have a Bonus Activity with suggestions for exploring additional Bible passages.

EXTENDING THE CONVERSATION

- *Looking Back*—Revisits the notes from "IQ" (Insights & Questions) Time collected at the beginning of the session. This is usually a good opportunity to affirm what has been learned and sometimes to sharpen questions that the participants will want to keep in mind going forward.

- *Looking Ahead*—Previews the subject to be covered in the next chapter and session. You can share the brief instructions provided to "prime the pump" before participants read the next chapter and prepare for the next session.

REPRODUCIBLE SESSION HANDOUTS

These are provided to you for each session in case you want the learners to have the questions that accompany the activities of the study (Join the Conversation and Open Scripture). They also include the assignment for the upcoming session.

MAKE THE COURSE YOUR OWN

While the Conversation Starters, Activities, Bible Passages, and Bonus Activities are designed to reinforce and build on each other, please feel free to tailor or adapt these pieces to fit the needs and goals of your group. For example, you may anticipate spending extra time on a particular Activity and decide to spend less time on the Bible Passage that week, or vice versa. The Leader Guide sessions are just that—guides with information and suggestions to equip you to lead and facilitate each week's study. You are and remain the leader of this study, and you can and should exercise your discretion in how to use the material provided. So after reading the Leader Guide, feel free to make this course your own.

Advice and Counsel

Be assured that you have everything you need to lead this course of study effectively. By reading through the Leader Guide ahead of time and doing some minimal preparation, you can be confident of facilitating a rewarding and enjoyable learning session for your participants. Below are several suggestions for enhancing that experience.

- *Making Sense of the Cross* is the main resource for each of the participants. The material in your Leader Guide is provided only to you. While you may want occasionally to read aloud or otherwise share some of the material in the Leader Guide (the chapter summaries, for instance), you will more often profit by encouraging participants to read from and engage the material directly from their books.

- *Questions are central to this course.* It will be helpful at the very beginning and throughout the course to remind people that there are no dumb questions, that we learn from the questions we have and that others ask, and that questions are, indeed, the mark of a curious and eager mind. You all have a great deal to teach and learn from each other; reminding participants of your confidence in this will only help develop trust and support within the group.

- ***Don't be afraid of silence.*** Sometimes one of the most difficult things about leading a study of any kind is enduring the silence that often comes immediately after you ask a question. As the leader, you have had time to think through the questions ahead of time. Participants, however, may not have thought of these questions before and are using this time to formulate their answers. What may seem like a very long time to you probably does not seem that long to the participants. So don't feel the need to fill the silences, but allow those to be "holy times" of contemplation in a world where such time is scarce.

- ***Pay attention to building relationships.*** As important as the material covered in each session may be, the relationships you are developing with each other around your shared interest in Scripture and the cross is more important. Always make room for catching up and checking in with each other, and always allow time and space for people to share their thoughts and questions, insights, and concerns. The time you spend with each other in conversation and prayer will always be time well spent.

- ***Conversations about faith, and certainly about the cross and resurrection, sometimes engender strong emotions in people.*** Even those who have not actively participated in a Bible study or attended worship in some time or read a Bible in years may be surprised at how strong their opinions about the cross are. Don't be caught off guard if people in your group disagree about various aspects of the cross or the Christian faith. (For instance, some may believe that there is only one way to understand the cross.) When such emotions or sentiments are expressed, try not to be defensive. Rather, consider the following steps in replying to a difficult or impassioned question:

    1. Honor the questioner by listening carefully to the question. You may want to try to reflect back what you are hearing to make sure you understand the participant correctly (for example, "It sounds like you are saying that it is very important to you that the cross be understood in this particular way").
    2. Acknowledge the validity of the question.
    3. Remind all participants that intelligent and faithful people can and will disagree with each other from time to time on these kinds of issues. Such disagreements do not signal a lack of faith.
    4. With the permission of the questioner, turn the question over to the larger group for discussion so that all participants have an opportunity to share their insights and similar questions.
    5. Work to maintain a level of respect and consideration for each other, rooted in a shared faith in the God we know in Jesus. Remember that this is more important than "resolving" differences.

A FINAL WORD

I am very excited for what you, as the leader and facilitator of the group, will learn by playing this role, and I am grateful for the service you are rendering your co-learners. Thank you for your time, effort, and good faith. Even more, thank God for you.

David Lose, author
Making Sense of the Cross

Session Schedules and Variations

The *Making Sense of the Cross* course is flexible to fit a variety of settings and timeframes. Use the following charts to guide your session planning. *Making Sense of the Cross* contains many rich theological concepts and opportunities for exploration and discussion. As you review the session materials, you may want to consider extending this course so the group can engage in deeper conversations with each other and with the Bible.

We include the times for a 60-minute session in our session discussions that follow.

	45 MINUTES	60 MINUTES	90 MINUTES	120 MINUTES
GATHER	5	10	15	15
JOIN THE CONVERSATION	20	20	35	50
OPEN SCRIPTURE	15	20	30	45
EXTENDING THE CONVERSATION	5	10	10	10

Depending on your desired emphasis, you may want to adjust the times given to each part of the session.

Using a Retreat Format

Consider a retreat option if you want to focus concentrated time on *Making Sense of the Cross*. You might even consider using this as a leadership retreat for your council and other congregational leaders. If you do plan to do the course in a retreat setting, you will greatly benefit by having the participants read the book *Making Sense of the Cross* before the retreat begins. Order copies and hand them out to retreat participants at least two weeks in advance if possible.

If you use this course in a retreat setting, you may want to meet one or more times after the retreat to continue your conversations and put the Take It with You options into practice.

Day 1: Friday

5:30 p.m.	*Supper*
6:30–8:00 p.m.	*Session 1*
8:00–8:10 p.m.	*Break*
8:10–9:40 p.m.	*Session 2*

Day 2: Saturday

7:30 a.m.	*Breakfast*
8:45–10:15 a.m.	*Session 3*
10:15–10:25 a.m.	*Break*
10:25–11:55 a.m.	*Session 4*
Noon–1:00 p.m.	*Lunch*
1:00–2:30 p.m.	*Session 5*
2:30–2:40 p.m.	*Break*
2:40–4:10 p.m.	*Session 6*
4:10–4:25 p.m.	*Closing Prayer and Departure*

Covenant

We agree to join with others in this study and discussion of the cross and Christian faith together.

It is our understanding that . . .
- No prior knowledge of the Bible or theology is expected or required.
- Members will not be forced to speak if we are not comfortable doing so.
- Group members are expected to respect each other's views.

We will do our best to . . .
- Read the study material in advance of each session.
- Make attendance at sessions a high priority.
- Share our ideas in the sessions, speaking as we are able.
- Tolerate the opinions and ideas of others.
- Keep personal things spoken in our time together confidential.
- Respond as we are able to requests of the leader and the various coordinators.
- Pray for the group gathered for study.

Signature _____ Date _____

Roster of Group Members

Names	Email / Phone Number / Address

Invitation Letter

Dear _____ ,

A group of us will be gathering soon to begin an exciting study called *Making Sense of the Cross.* There is no expectation that you have certain prior knowledge of the Bible or theology. Just bring your questions and openness to talk about matters of the cross and resurrection of Jesus. I would be very pleased if you could join us.

We will gather on _____ at _____ .
                                    [day and date]   *[location]*

We are meeting at _____ , and will plan to meet for about _____ minutes.
                                [time]

Copies of the book used in the study are available in the church office. If you plan to join us, you will find it very helpful to have read the Introduction and first chapter of the book. But even if you haven't read the book ahead of time, come anyway.

It should be a very relaxed first gathering. I'll call you in the next few days to see if you have any questions.

Talk to you soon!

In Christ,

session 1
A Man Hanging on a Tree

Prepare

FOCUS STATEMENT

If, as Christians confess, the cross is the place where we see God revealed most fully, then we need to reconsider all of our assumptions and statements about God in light of what happens to Jesus, the man "hanging on a tree."

CHAPTER OVERVIEW

Even though the cross stands at the center of our faith lives, we often don't pause to consider its meaning and significance. Perhaps because we see it almost everywhere—in churches; on signs and bumper stickers; worn as jewelry; used as imagery in art, film, and television—we forget what a powerful and even troubling image it was for the first Christians.

When you read the Bible carefully, however, you soon realize two important things about the cross. First, no one expected God's promised Messiah to be crucified. The very fact that Jesus died on a cross was at first a huge problem. If this is the way God chose to be revealed to the world, those early Christians reasoned, then they needed to rethink everything they thought they knew about God, the world, and their faith. In many ways, the whole New Testament is the attempt of those early believers to make sense of their Scriptures (what we now call the Old Testament) and their experience in light of the cross.

Second, we realize that even as the cross was unexpected, even more so was the resurrection—so unexpected, in fact, that no one in the four Gospels at first believes the message of Christ's resurrection. Sometimes this news creates fear, sometimes doubt, sometimes questions, but at first none of Jesus' disciples believes the good news. Noticing this helps us not only recognize how amazing the resurrection was and is, but also helps us to be patient with ourselves as we try to make sense of our lives in light of Jesus' cross and resurrection.

Over time, as the early Christians had more time to reflect on the cross, it shaped their reflections about Jesus' life and their own. One of the key insights they had regarding the cross was that it shapes all of our thinking and conversations about God. This can be challenging, as we often tend to think about God primarily in terms of the qualities or attributes we think God must have. That is, we think about God in terms of God being omnipotent ("all powerful"), omniscient ("all knowing"), all just, all holy, etc. These "all" qualities make sense to us, because God just seems "bigger" than anything we can imagine. But the challenge of thinking about God in terms of God's power and size is that we soon realize this God is so far beyond us that we lose all hope of knowing and being known by this God. Eventually, we realize that we cannot expect to connect with this kind of God and certainly can't expect to be found acceptable by this God. While God may be all holy, all just, all powerful, and all the rest, we most certainly are not.

This was just the struggle that engaged the life and work of a sixteenth-century monk by the name of Martin Luther. Luther became convinced of two things that still animate Christian faith, life, and theology today. First, the God of attributes—all holy, all just, etc.—can ultimately only terrify us because we will never measure up to such a God. Second, in the cross of Jesus we see another side of God—perhaps even a different God than we'd imagined altogether—revealed. This God is not only powerful but also vulnerable. This God is not only just but also forgiving. This God is not only all-knowing but loving. In fact, Luther suggests that we need to redefine what we mean by words like *power* and *justice* in light of what we see God actually do in Jesus—namely, come and proclaim a kingdom of forgiveness and love and then die for us on the cross.

In this way, the cross shapes all that we say and think about God, revealing to us a God we probably would never expect but recognize we desperately need. We will therefore begin our journey by looking at the four accounts of Jesus' death and resurrection in the four Gospels.

BEFORE YOU BEGIN

The curious thing about the cross is that as central as it is to the Christian faith, as much as we hear it referenced, we don't really talk about it all that much. That is, we don't talk about what it means, what it accomplishes, why Jesus had to die, or whether Jesus had to die. So take a few moments and ask yourself how much you really know about the cross. Could you explain to someone who didn't know much about Christianity why the cross is important? If not, what questions are surfaced by this exercise? What do you wonder about? What might some of the participants in your group wonder about? Keep in mind that all the questions that arise are good questions, and your job isn't to answer them but to provide a space for them to be voiced.

SESSION INSTRUCTIONS

1. Read chapter one in *Making Sense of the Cross* and this Leader Guide session completely. Highlight or underline any portions you wish to emphasize with the group. Note also any bonus activities you want to do.

> **TIP**
>
> Giving voice to our questions or even doubts about the meaning of the cross and resurrection may be challenging for many Christians, as it is something we feel we should "just know." Stress early and often that there are no dumb questions and that one of the reasons we may not have reflected much on the cross is precisely because it is considered so central. Remind participants that the cross is so important that it deserves not just our attention but also our questions, as we learn the most when we acknowledge what we're curious about, wonder about, and question.

> **TIP**
>
> If possible, distribute copies of *Making Sense of the Cross* to participants before the first session and invite them to read the introduction and chapter one, "A Man Hanging on a Tree." Be prepared to recap the chapter for any group members who did not have the book or were not able to do the advance reading.

2. If you plan to do any special activities, collect all the materials you'll need. Each session will call for chart paper and markers or another means to collect insights and questions.

FACILITATOR'S PRAYER

Spend some time in prayer for those who will be coming to this class, for yourself, and for the session ahead. If it is helpful, you may use this prayer as a guide:

Dear God, bless each one who comes to this study, and bless me as a leader. Open our ears, hearts, and minds so that we may come to know you more deeply as we learn together about you through our study and conversation about the death and resurrection of your Son, Jesus Christ. Amen.

Gather (10 minutes)

WELCOME AND CHECK-IN

Welcome the group. Small group study may be a new experience for some, and it is important for people to feel welcome and secure. Provide name tags and make time for introductions. Snacks, or even a meal together to celebrate this new venture, can help the group feel more comfortable.

SUPPLIES
- [ ] Name tags
- [ ] Pens
- [ ] Snacks or a meal (optional)
- [ ] Chart paper
- [ ] Markers
- [ ] Copies of *Making Sense of the Cross*

OPENING PRAYER

Dear God, we gather together with questions, hopes, and dreams. Some of these we can name; some are hard to put words to. But we trust that you know our needs and will use this time of study and conversation to help meet them. Bless our time together as we listen to and learn from each other, from Christians through the centuries, and from your Word, that we may grow in our relationship with you and each other. In Jesus' name we pray. Amen.

INSIGHTS AND QUESTIONS (IQ) TIME

Invite participants to share any insights they had while reading chapter one. List these insights on chart paper where all can see.

Ask the group to share any questions they have about what they read. Collect these on chart paper as well.

Set the lists aside so you can return to them at the end of the session.

TIP

Reassure group members that all questions and insights are welcome. There are no "wrong" questions or insights. If you go around the room to give everyone a chance to participate, make sure people know it's all right to "pass" or not offer an insight or question.

Session 1
A Man Hanging on a Tree

Join the Conversation (20 minutes)

VIDEO INTRODUCTION

Watch the video segment for session one. The course author will introduce the key concepts from the book and prepare the group for the activities that follow.

CONVERSATION STARTER

Read these quotations from chapter one of *Making Sense of the Cross*; then invite the participants to discuss the questions that follow.

> "When Jesus died, all the hopes his early followers had about him and for him died, too. The one they thought would redeem them, the one they'd called "Messiah" and "Son of God," was now dead. So when they experienced the resurrected Jesus—or, in the case of the Gospel writers, heard about the resurrected Jesus—they realized God was up to something they had never, ever expected. It took them a while—and I mean a long while—to figure it out, but ultimately they were convinced that Jesus' death and resurrection changed everything." (p. 12)

> "Because what you see in Jesus is what you get in God—I like that!—you need to rethink all the talk about God's attributes in light of what actually happens to Jesus. And once Luther did that he realized that the God we see in Jesus is quite different from the God-of-attributes he'd imagined. Luther says that this God—the one revealed in Jesus on the cross—is vulnerable rather than powerful, approachable rather than distant, and is someone you can count on receiving mercy and grace from rather than judgment. Ultimately, Luther observes, this God is the one who understands everything we go through because, in Jesus, God went through it all too, even death." (p. 20)

Discuss:
1. Put yourself in the place of Jesus' disciples during and just after his crucifixion. What are some emotions you might experience? How would this event affect your faith and your sense of the future?
2. Now imagine hearing that Jesus has been raised. How would you react? How would this affect your view of the cross and your ideas about how God works in the world?
3. What are some adjectives you might use to describe God? What kind of picture of God do these words offer? How are these words shaped by what you see in Jesus' cross and resurrection?
4. What difference does it make to remember that God, in Jesus, knows what it's like to be human?

SUPPLIES
- [ ] *Making Sense of the Cross* DVD
- [ ] TV and DVD player (or computer, projection system, and screen)
- [ ] Copies of *Making Sense of the Cross*
- [ ] Session handout (p. 18)

TIP
Preview the DVD segment and take some notes. Set up DVD equipment before the session begins. If you will not be showing the DVD, summarize the "Chapter Overview" for the group.

TIP
Encourage the group to follow along in their books as you (or volunteers) read each quotation.

> **TIP**
>
> It may take a little while for people to move beyond thinking about the typical places where they've seen a cross, but once they get going, they may be surprised at just how many crosses they have seen. Be patient, invite them to be creative, and allow a little extra time if folks need it for brainstorming.

ACTIVITY: COUNTING CROSSES

Have participants form small groups of three or four. Invite them to brainstorm a list of places where they've seen crosses. Encourage them to think beyond crosses inside or outside church buildings, in jewelry, and on church signs. Where have they seen the cross used as a symbol in movies or television or advertisements? (Ask them to be as concrete as possible in their responses—which movie, what do they think the cross meant, and so on.) After the small groups have shared the results of their brainstorming, ask them to discuss what they think about all these crosses. What does the cross mean in our popular culture? In our religious culture? In our daily lives? Is there one meaning or many, and how does that shape their thinking about the cross?

Open Scripture (20 minutes)

1 CORINTHIANS 1:18—2:2

This passage is considered one of the central places in the writings of the Apostle Paul. Here he expresses his "theology of the cross" as he describes how unexpected, even startling, the cross was.

Discuss:
1. What does Paul mean by saying that "the message about the cross is foolishness" and a "stumbling block"? What about the cross is startling, scandalous, or troubling to you?
2. God was at work through the cross. Why was this so unexpected for those living in Paul's time? In what ways is it unexpected or surprising in our own time?
3. Why do you think Paul links the "lowliness" of the cross to the humble natures of the people to whom he is writing?

SUPPLIES
- [ ] Bibles
- [ ] Session handout
- [ ] Copies of *Making Sense of the Cross*
- [ ] Scissors
- [ ] Glue sticks
- [ ] Small sheets of cardstock or construction paper
- [ ] Old magazines

BONUS ACTIVITY: WHEN I THINK OF GOD . . .

Have available scissors, glue sticks, small sheets of cardstock or construction paper, and a variety of old magazines. Invite each person to page through the magazines and cut out pictures that help them imagine what God is like, then glue the images onto cardstock or construction paper to create a collage. Encourage volunteers to show their collages to the group and share what the various images mean to them.

> **TIP**
>
> Encourage people to save their collages so you can revisit them at the end of this course.

Extending the Conversation (10 minutes)

LOOKING BACK

Review the lists of insights and questions from IQ Time. Which insights and questions have been answered or clarified? Which remain unanswered? Ask participants to share additional questions or insights that have surfaced during your time together.

LOOKING AHEAD

Direct the group to the session handout and review ways to prepare for your next meeting.

1. Before reading chapter two, write down some of your thoughts about the passion narrative—the story of Jesus' crucifixion. What scenes do you remember most vividly? How would you summarize the plot?
2. Read at least *one* of the four Gospel accounts of the crucifixion and resurrection: Mark 14:26—16:8; Matthew 26:30—28:20; Luke 22:39—24:53; John 18:1—20:31. Compare your recollection of this story with the Gospel account you read.
3. Read chapter two in *Making Sense of the Cross*—"Portraits and Perspectives."
4. Jot down any insights or questions you have after reading the chapter. In particular, pay attention to your reaction to the ideas that (a) the Gospels tell complementary but distinct stories of the cross, and (b) each author is making a distinct confession of faith that the church believed was important to preserve.

Optional: Rent and watch one of the many "life of Jesus" movies, for example, *The Greatest Story Ever Told* (MGM, 1965), *Jesus of Nazareth* (Lions Gate, 1977), *The Passion of the Christ* (20th Century Fox, 2004). How is the cross portrayed? What scenes from the Gospel account(s) that you read did the director choose to include or leave out?

SUPPLIES
- ☐ Chart paper from IQ Time
- ☐ Copies of *Making Sense of the Cross*
- ☐ Session handout

TIP

You can help to enliven conversation next week by making sure that each of the Gospel accounts is being read by at least one person so that members can compare and contrast the accounts they read.

Session 1 Handout

A Man Hanging on a Tree

FOCUS STATEMENT

If, as Christians confess, the cross is the place where we see God revealed most fully, then we need to reconsider all of our assumptions and statements about God in light of what happens to Jesus, the man "hanging on a tree."

CONVERSATION STARTER

Discuss:
1. Put yourself in the place of Jesus' disciples during and just after his crucifixion. What are some emotions you might experience? How would this event affect your faith and your sense of the future?
2. Now imagine hearing that Jesus has been raised. How would you react? How would this affect your view of the cross and your ideas about how God works in the world?
3. What are some adjectives you might use to describe God? What kind of picture of God do these words offer? How are these words shaped by what you see in Jesus' cross and resurrection?
4. What difference does it make to remember that God, in Jesus, knows what it's like to be human?

1 CORINTHIANS 1:18—2:2

Discuss:
1. What does Paul mean by saying that "the message about the cross is foolishness" and a "stumbling block"? What about the cross is startling, scandalous, or troubling to you?
2. God was at work through the cross. Why was this so unexpected for those living in Paul's time? In what ways is it unexpected or surprising in our own time?
3. Why do you think Paul links the "lowliness" of the cross to the humble natures of the people to whom he is writing?

LOOKING AHEAD

1. Before reading chapter two, write down some of your thoughts about the passion narrative—the story of Jesus' crucifixion. What scenes do you remember most vividly? How would you summarize the plot?
2. Read at least *one* of the four Gospel accounts of the crucifixion and resurrection: Mark 14:26—16:8; Matthew 26:30—28:20; Luke 22:39—24:53; John 18:1—20:31. Compare your recollection of this story with the Gospel account you read.
3. Read chapter two in *Making Sense of the Cross*—"Portraits and Perspectives."
4. Jot down any insights or questions you have after reading the chapter. In particular, pay attention to your reaction to the ideas that (a) the Gospels tell complementary but distinct stories of the cross, and (b) each author is making a distinct confession of faith that the church believed was important to preserve.

session 2
Portraits and Perspectives

Prepare

FOCUS STATEMENT

The Christian church affirmed that the four distinct portraits of Jesus found in the four Gospels help us see and understand the truth of what God was accomplishing through Jesus better than any single portrayal could, as each one offers a unique glimpse into the importance and meaning of his life, death, and resurrection.

CHAPTER OVERVIEW

Most of us grew up thinking about the story of Jesus as *one* story, a unified and consistent whole the Bible tells about his life, ministry, death, and resurrection. On one level, that makes a lot of sense, as the story we hold in our heads has come from reading and hearing the Gospel stories of Jesus over many years. In addition, we have probably seen one or more movies or plays about the life of Jesus that have helped us stitch together a coherent, cohesive narrative. It's therefore natural, understandable, and useful to combine the various Gospel stories into one.

At another level, however, it's also important to recognize that each of the four biblical Gospels tells a distinct story of Jesus in order to make a particular confession of faith about his importance. When we read the Gospel stories closely, we soon realize that while they share many similar elements—characters, overall plot, etc.—they are also quite distinct and contain numerous different details. Some of those differences are relatively small—did the disciples fall asleep in Gethsemane one time (as reported by Luke), three times (as reported by Matthew and Mark), or not at all (as John offers no such report)? Some are much more significant—was the Friday on which Jesus died the Passover (as in Mark, Luke, and Matthew) or the Day of Preparation (the day before Passover, as in John)?

In each case, it's helpful to keep in mind that the author is choosing, adapting, and arranging elements from stories the Christian community told about Jesus in order to offer a distinct portrait of, and perspective on, Jesus' life, death, and resurrection. The Gospel writers, that is, are all making confessions of faith about who Jesus is and why he matters. They write hoping that by reading their confessions, we might also confess faith in Jesus (see John 20:30-31).

> **TIP**
>
> It may be challenging for some to acknowledge that the Gospels tell different—sometimes very different!—stories about Jesus. It's therefore helpful to stress that we are not trying to figure out which one is "right" but to hear the distinct confession of each author. Given this opportunity, most Christians come not only to recognize but also to appreciate the distinct portrayal and confession each author offers.

When reading one of the Gospel accounts of Jesus, our task is therefore not to figure out "which one is right" but rather to appreciate and understand what the author is trying to confess. Members of the early Christian church also recognized that the Gospels told similar but distinct stories about Jesus and came to believe that by holding the four distinct Gospels in tension, Christians actually had a better, richer understanding of the truth of what God was and is accomplishing through Jesus. We can therefore gain from understanding some of the distinctive contributions each of the Gospels makes to our picture of Jesus.

Mark, writer of the earliest Gospel, is probably writing to a Christian community that had recently gone through a period of intense struggle or suffering, perhaps resulting from persecution or from the Jewish-Roman war that culminated in the destruction of the Jerusalem Temple. Mark's story of Jesus, therefore, focuses on Jesus' humanity and, in particular, his suffering and his faithfulness. Mark, we believe, wants to encourage those who had suffered by showing that Jesus understands their suffering because he also suffered much. Mark hopes to encourage his community to be faithful amid their struggles, and he wants to make sure that those who may have turned away from the faith know that they are welcome to return. Mark portrays the disciples as often misunderstanding and ultimately failing Jesus to remind us that anyone can be a disciple and has an opportunity to return to the faith.

Matthew, the longest of the Gospels, draws heavily from Mark. Matthew is most likely writing to an audience made up largely of believers who had formerly been members of a Jewish synagogue. For this reason, Matthew is particularly interested in showing how Jesus fulfills prophecies about Israel's future Messiah and how similar he is to great figures in Israel's history like Moses. Jesus, like Moses, is very much a teacher in Matthew's Gospel, showing his disciples—then and now—what it means to be his followers. At times, Matthew's interest in demonstrating that Jesus is the true Messiah of Israel leads him to portray those Jews who didn't accept Jesus—particularly the Pharisees—in a very bad light. While that may have been relatively harmless when the Gospel was first written and Christians were in the minority, some of those passages were used to do great harm when Christians became the majority. It's important for us to be aware of both why Matthew described the story of Jesus in this way and what kind of damage this has sometimes done.

Luke also draws from Mark's account and shares a collection of Jesus' parables with Matthew. But he writes for a community that is made up of Jews and Gentiles from around the first-century Mediterranean world. Luke's Gospel is also the first half of a two-volume work telling the story both of Jesus and the early church. His second book, The Acts of the Apostles, therefore builds on what he tells us in the Gospel. Because of Luke's interest in the spread of the gospel beyond Jerusalem, he is interested in demonstrating that all people are invited by

Jesus into the kingdom of God. Luke's portrayal of Jesus emphasizes Jesus' compassion, his role as a healer, and his innocence.

John is the most distinct of the Gospels, sharing a basic outline of Jesus' ministry, death, and resurrection, but varying significantly in terms of the details he offers. John is probably writing to a community of formerly Jewish Christians who have experienced great struggles with the rest of the Jewish community. John therefore writes to reassure his audience that Jesus is, indeed, the true Messiah and that he is powerful enough to save them amid their difficulties. For this reason, he portrays Jesus as strong, confident, faithful, and always in control. The cross, according to John, is not a moment of darkness and defeat. Rather, it is the place and hour where we see God reveal God's victory and triumph.

By reading and holding in faithful tension these four distinct accounts, we not only will find that different elements of Jesus' life and character may speak to us at different times in our own lives, but we will also gain a fuller sense of the truth of God's accomplishment through the life, ministry, death, and resurrection of Jesus.

BEFORE YOU BEGIN

It may be helpful for you to consider your own upbringing and history when it comes to the story of Jesus. When did you realize that there are important and helpful differences among the Gospels? It may have been years ago or as you were preparing to lead this class. How did you feel about this realization? What was challenging? What was helpful?

SESSION INSTRUCTIONS

1. Read chapter two in *Making Sense of the Cross* and this Leader Guide session completely. Highlight or underline any portions you wish to emphasize with the group. Note also any bonus activities you want to do.
2. As always, having a whiteboard or newsprint available will be helpful. If you plan to do any special activities, check to see what materials you'll need, if any.

FACILITATOR'S PRAYER

Spend some time in prayer for those who will be coming to this class, for yourself, and for the session ahead. If it is helpful, you may use this prayer as a guide:

Dear God, bless each one who comes to this study, and bless me as a leader. Help us to hear the distinct and bold confession of faith contained in each of the Gospels, so that we may grow in our faith, understanding and appreciating more deeply all that you have accomplished through the life, death, and resurrection of Jesus. Amen.

> **TIP**
>
> If you have time, it might be valuable to read the four passion accounts: Mark 14:26—16:8; Matthew 26:30—28:20; Luke 22:39—24:53; John 18:1—20:31. Read these side by side, if possible, and highlight some of the important "tell-tale" details that stick out to you in each one. Why did you choose those details? What do they tell you about the particular confession of faith each author seeks to make?

Gather (10 minutes)

SUPPLIES
- [ ] Name tags
- [ ] Pens
- [ ] Snacks or a meal (optional)
- [ ] Chart paper
- [ ] Markers
- [ ] Copies of *Making Sense of the Cross*

TIP

In these first few sessions together, it may be helpful to again remind group members that all questions and insights are welcome. There are no "wrong" questions or insights. And, if you go around the room to give everyone a chance to participate, make sure people know it's all right to "pass" or not offer an insight or question.

WELCOME AND CHECK-IN

Welcome the group. Take special care to recognize and welcome any new participants. Take time to ask if anyone has had an additional insight or question about the previous session and conversation that he or she would like to share.

OPENING PRAYER

Dear God, from the beginning there have been men and women so gripped by their experience of your love that they had to confess. Among these are your servants Matthew, Mark, Luke, and John. Let the testimony of these early proclaimers of the gospel strengthen our own faith. And guide us in our reading, listening, and speaking, so that when we hear the stories of Jesus' cross and resurrection, we might realize anew just how much you love us. This we pray in Jesus' name. Amen.

INSIGHTS AND QUESTIONS (IQ) TIME

Invite participants to share any insights they had while reading chapter two. List these insights on chart paper where all can see.

Ask the group to share any questions they have about what they read. Collect these on chart paper as well.

Set the lists aside so you can return to them at the end of the session.

Join the Conversation (20 minutes)

SUPPLIES
- [ ] *Making Sense of the Cross* DVD
- [ ] TV and DVD player (or computer, projection system, and screen)
- [ ] Copies of *Making Sense of the Cross*
- [ ] Session handout (p. 26)

TIP

Preview the DVD segment and take some notes. Set up DVD equipment before the session begins. If you will not be showing the DVD, summarize the "Chapter Overview" for the group.

VIDEO INTRODUCTION

Watch the video segment for session two. The course author will introduce the key concepts from the book and prepare the group for the activities that follow.

CONVERSATION STARTER

Read these quotations from chapter two of *Making Sense of the Cross*; then invite the participants to discuss the questions that follow:

> "The four Gospel writers were not offering these confessions in general but to specific communities of faith. And so each Gospel starts with a particular group of Christians in mind and tries to tell the story in a way that makes sense to them, while also addressing some of the particular concerns, problems, and setbacks that specific community was having." (p. 33)

> "Each difference we encounter functions like a clue to the meaning of the larger story the author is trying to tell. So when we come across a difference between, for instance, Luke and Mark, the question isn't, 'Which one is right?' but instead, 'What's Luke trying to tell us with this different detail?'" (p. 34)

Discuss:
1. Before taking this class, had you noticed some of the differences between the Gospel stories of Jesus? How does it help to think of these differences as clues to the distinct confession each evangelist is making?
2. What do you think of the early church's decision to retain four distinct Gospels? Do you think it would be clearer and simpler to have just one harmonized version, or do you think we gain a richer, more three-dimensional view of Jesus through the different perspectives?
3. At this point, does one of the four passion stories appeal to you more than the others? What is it about this story that speaks to you here and now? Can you imagine some of the others being helpful to you as you face different circumstances?

TIP

Encourage the group to follow along in their books as you (or volunteers) read each quotation.

ACTIVITY: GOSPEL ENACTMENTS

Divide the group into four teams. Each team is given the name of one of the four evangelists—Matthew, Mark, Luke, or John—and is asked to silently "act out" what they think is the central description, portrayal, and confession of faith the author is trying to make about Jesus. Give teams five minutes to discuss how they want to bring to life the particular perspective of their evangelist and then share their performances. The other groups are invited to guess which evangelist's story the performing team is enacting. Even after a couple of performances—when the guessing becomes easier!—still have each remaining group share its enactment of the Gospel. After all teams are done, discuss the choices each team made to represent the confession of their evangelist.

TIP

For some folks, learning that the Gospel stories don't agree on all the details may be new. The more time they can spend reading the Gospels themselves and talking about the distinct confession of faith they see each evangelist making, the easier and more enjoyable noticing these differences will become.

SUPPLIES
- ☐ Bibles
- ☐ Session handout
- ☐ Copies of *Making Sense of the Cross*
- ☐ Newsprint or whiteboard
- ☐ Markers

Open Scripture (20 minutes)

MARK 14:32-52; MATTHEW 26:36-56; LUKE 22:39-53; JOHN 18:1-11

Read these four stories of Jesus' betrayal aloud. After each one, ask these three questions and record brief answers on newsprint or a whiteboard: What are the primary details that you notice? How is Jesus portrayed? What confession about Jesus is the author trying to make?

Discuss:
1. Which of these accounts is most familiar to you? Which is most unfamiliar?
2. What details most surprised you? Why do you think you hadn't noticed them before?
3. Which account speaks to you most clearly on this day or at this time in your life? Why do you think that is?

BONUS ACTIVITY: TIMES AND SEASONS

Having read and discussed in some detail each of the four Gospel accounts, now brainstorm about different situations or circumstances in which hearing the particular confession of each evangelist might be helpful. For instance, with Mark it might be during times of suffering, or when you have real doubts about God's presence in your life. Take a few moments to compare the lists. Are there any seasons or circumstances in life that are left out? How do the Gospels address these situations?

Extending the Conversation (10 minutes)

LOOKING BACK

Review the lists made during IQ Time. Which insights and questions have been answered or clarified? Which remain unanswered? Ask participants to share additional questions or insights that have surfaced during your time together.

LOOKING AHEAD

Direct the group to the session handout and review ways to prepare for your next meeting:
1. Before reading chapter three, write down some of your thoughts about sin. What do you think of when you think of sin? Is your reaction to this word and concept largely positive, negative, apprehensive, or something else?
2. Read chapter three in *Making Sense of the Cross*—"Ransom and Victory."
3. Jot down any insights or questions you have after reading the chapter. In particular, pay attention to your reaction to the idea that the cross represents God's entering into the struggle to redeem us from the devil. Does this make sense or seem helpful? Why or why not?

Optional: After reading chapter three in *Making Sense of the Cross*, watch either the film version of C.S. Lewis' *The Lion, the Witch, and the Wardrobe* (Walt Disney Pictures, 2005) or *Star Wars* (20th Century Fox, 1977). How does the imagery employed in the film help make more vivid the ransom and victory theory of atonement?

SUPPLIES
- ☐ Chart paper from IQ Time
- ☐ Copies of *Making Sense of the Cross*
- ☐ Session handout

TIP

You may wish to keep the IQ lists and review them as you prepare for the next session.

Session 2 Handout

Portraits and Perspectives

FOCUS STATEMENT

The Christian church affirmed that the four distinct portraits of Jesus found in the four Gospels help us see and understand the truth of what God was accomplishing through Jesus better than any single portrayal could, as each one offers a unique glimpse into the importance and meaning of his life, death, and resurrection.

CONVERSATION STARTER

Discuss:
1. Before taking this class, had you noticed some of the differences between the Gospel stories of Jesus? How does it help to think of these differences as clues to the distinct confession each evangelist is making?
2. What do you think of the early church's decision to retain four distinct Gospels? Do you think it would be clearer and simpler to have just one harmonized version, or do you think we gain a richer, more three-dimensional view of Jesus through the different perspectives?
3. At this point, does one of the four passion stories appeal to you more than the others? What is it about this story that speaks to you here and now? Can you imagine some of the others being helpful to you as you face different circumstances?

MARK 14:32-52; MATTHEW 26:36-56; LUKE 22:39-53; JOHN 18:1-11

Discuss:
1. Which of these accounts is most familiar to you? Which is most unfamiliar?
2. What details most surprised you? Why do you think you hadn't noticed them before?
3. Which account speaks to you most clearly on this day or at this time in your life? Why do you think that is?

LOOKING AHEAD

1. Before reading chapter three, write down some of your thoughts about sin. What do you think of when you think of sin? Is your reaction to this word and concept largely positive, negative, apprehensive, or something else?
2. Read chapter three in *Making Sense of the Cross*—"Ransom and Victory."
3. Jot down any insights or questions you have after reading the chapter. In particular, pay attention to your reaction to the idea that the cross represents God's entering into the struggle to redeem us from the devil. Does this make sense or seem helpful? Why or why not?

Session 2 Handout: *Making Sense of the Cross*. Permission is granted to reproduce this page for local use. Copyright © Augsburg Fortress, 2011.

session 3
Ransom and Victory

Prepare

FOCUS STATEMENT

The theory or model of atonement that was popular for much of the first thousand years in Christian history emphasizes the titanic struggle between God and Satan for the fate of humanity, a struggle that culminates in God's triumph through the cross and resurrection of Jesus.

CHAPTER OVERVIEW

When we looked at the four Gospel accounts of the story of Jesus, we discovered that each makes a distinct and valuable confession of faith about the meaning of his life, ministry, death, and resurrection. For this reason, we found it important not to collapse these different perspectives but to try to hear the unique "theology of the cross" that each one offered.

Because the evangelists—the authors of the Gospels—tell a story about Jesus rather than write an essay about him, their theology is *implicit*—that is, embedded in the story itself. That's why we read each one carefully, paying attention to the details of the actual narrative. Later theologians would read all four Gospels together and try to offer more *explicit* theories or models about how God achieves atonement through the cross.

Atonement literally means what it says: *at-one-ment*, making something that was broken whole again. The first theory of atonement became popular within a century or two after the events of Jesus' life described in the four Gospels, and it remained popular for nearly a thousand years. The key element of this theory is that God is engaged in a huge struggle with the devil for the fate and destiny of humanity, a struggle that everyday Christians can feel played out in their lives as they suffer oppression and resist evil.

This understanding of the cross draws heavily upon the story of the fall of Adam and Eve from a state of grace to a state of sin. Because Adam and Eve sin—that is, disobey God's will—their relationship with God is broken and they are now under the rule of Satan, the tempter (and, in some stories, rebellious angel) who has charge over the fates of all those who disobey God. But God still loves God's wayward children and does not want to surrender them to the fate of eternal separation from God under the power of the devil. For this reason, God becomes human in the person of Jesus and enters into the story and struggle in a more personal, direct, and dramatic way.

> **TIP**
>
> The "Ransom and Victory" theory of atonement is the most "mythic" or "cosmic" theory of atonement, which is why it may be easier to see and understand its themes as they find expression in stories like *The Lion, the Witch, and the Wardrobe* and movies like *Star Wars*. It may be helpful to review the primary contours of the theory and explore what questions you have about it. Keep in mind that these stories, and others, can help make the elements of the theory a little more concrete.

At this point, there are two main variations in the story of how God achieves redemption through the cross. In one variation, God tricks the devil. God's divinity is disguised in the humanity of Jesus, so that when Satan claims Jesus in death, he overreaches himself—as the perfect Son of God is not subject to his rule of death—and so the devil must surrender Jesus and all other humanity with him.

In another version of this theory, God offers Jesus as a ransom or exchange for all humanity. Satan eagerly accepts, believing that if he has God's Son in his clutches, he will wield great power over God as well, but he doesn't realize that he is not capable of containing the power and innocence of the Son. When Jesus defeats death by rising from the dead, he makes it possible for all those who believe in him also to escape eternal death. The cross, therefore, becomes the place of God's great victory over death and the devil.

The great appeal and strength of this theory of atonement is that it emphasizes that God is not unmoved by our struggles and fate, but instead enters into our lives to contest with the devil for our very lives. Developed during a time when Christians were often oppressed or persecuted, this theory spoke clear words of encouragement that God is fighting alongside all those who suffer and are oppressed by the forces of evil. While particularly popular in the first centuries of Christianity, this view of atonement has continued to appeal to people who suffer oppression, addiction, abuse, and many other afflictions, as it reminds us that we are not alone in our afflictions.

The great shortcoming of this theory for many people is that it seems a little too mythic or cosmic to connect to their everyday lives. Many Christians living in the modern world have difficulty relating to scenarios about God bargaining with, paying, or tricking the devil. It's a worldview that often does not seem to match our own.

BEFORE YOU BEGIN

In this chapter, we will consider the first of three theories of atonement—that is, models or explanations about how God restores what is broken in our relationship with God. Each of these models has helped Christians living at different times and places to understand what God has accomplished through Jesus' cross and resurrection. We should, therefore, read them first *sympathetically*, trying to understand what is helpful about them. We will then also read them *critically*, attempting to voice where they seem less helpful. It may be useful to remind yourself and the members of the group that even those theories they don't agree with will have helpful elements, just as those theories that most appeal to them will have shortcomings. Further, different theories may appeal more or less to different members of the group. That is okay; there is no one ultimate theory or model that can explain everything God accomplished in Christ.

Session 3
Ransom and Victory

SESSION INSTRUCTIONS

1. Read chapter three in *Making Sense of the Cross* and this Leader Guide session completely. Highlight or underline any portions you wish to emphasize with the group. Note also any bonus activities you want to do.
2. As always, having a whiteboard or newsprint available will be helpful. If you plan to do any special activities, check to see what materials you'll need, if any.

FACILITATOR'S PRAYER

Spend some time in prayer for those who will be coming to this class, for yourself, and for the session ahead. If it is helpful, you may use this prayer as a guide:

Dear God, bless each one who comes to this study, and bless me as a leader. Help us to see in this theory your great commitment to win us back from death at any cost, and help us to appreciate why this message has been so important to Christians through the ages. Amen.

Gather (10 minutes)

WELCOME AND CHECK-IN

Welcome the group. Take special care to recognize and welcome any new participants. Take time to ask if anyone has had an additional insight or question about the previous session and conversation that he or she would like to share.

OPENING PRAYER

Dear God, you have created us to enjoy life with you forever, and you desire only good for us. Yet we have regularly fallen short of your goals and hopes for us and have too often made a mess of our lives and this world. Save us from the bondage of sin and the dominion of the evil one, that we might be renewed in faith, hope, and courage. Amen.

INSIGHTS AND QUESTIONS (IQ) TIME

Invite participants to share any insights they had while reading chapter three. List these insights on chart paper where all can see.

Ask the group to share any questions they have about what they read. Collect these on chart paper as well.

Set the lists aside so you can return to them at the end of the session.

SUPPLIES
- ☐ Name tags
- ☐ Pens
- ☐ Snacks or a meal (optional)
- ☐ Chart paper
- ☐ Markers
- ☐ Copies of *Making Sense of the Cross*

TIP

Be prepared for more questions than insights. This view of the cross is perhaps most distant from our everyday life and view of the world. Reassure participants that it's okay if they didn't understand everything. Collecting these questions and working through the exercises below will help.

Join the Conversation (20 minutes)

SUPPLIES
- ☐ *Making Sense of the Cross* DVD
- ☐ TV and DVD player (or computer, projection system, and screen)
- ☐ Copies of *Making Sense of the Cross*
- ☐ Session handout (p. 33)

VIDEO INTRODUCTION

Watch the video segment for session three. The course author will introduce the key concepts from the book and prepare the group for the activities that follow.

CONVERSATION STARTER

Read these quotations from chapter three of *Making Sense of the Cross*; then invite the participants to discuss the questions that follow:

> "Some Christians have tended to make the way they understand the cross the absolute and only way any good Christian can understand the cross. And I think that's a mistake…. Because, as we just said, the best stories are those that can only be *experienced*. They can't be fully explained. Various interpretations of the cross are helpful, but no single one of them fully exhausts the potential for the passion narratives to have an effect on people, to move them to faith in the God made known through Jesus." (p. 81)

> "Atonement actually means just what it says: it's concerned with the question of how you repair or restore something that is broken. So, quite literally, it means to be "at one" or "in accord" with someone, or "at-one-ment." So when you make atonement for something, you are doing something to repair a broken relationship." (pp. 82-83)

> "Christians, especially those living under oppression, have more recently recovered the symbolism of the classic theory of atonement as well. Sometimes it might be economic or political oppression, while at other times it might be because they are the minority religious group in their homeland. Or it might be that they are struggling with addiction or trapped in an abusive relationship. Christians in any of these situations might see these forces of oppression and misery as linked to death and the devil, and they may feel very much that they are being held hostage by the forces of evil. So the imagery of Jesus taking on their situation, their death, and struggling to free them is pretty powerful." (p. 96)

Discuss:
1. What do you find comforting—or uncomfortable—about the idea that the cross is too big for any one theory or model of atonement to explain? What might still be helpful about knowing and understanding several different theories of atonement?
2. When have you experienced "atonement"—that is, the healing or restoration of a relationship that was broken? How might recalling these experiences help you approach our discussions of the cross?

TIP

Preview the DVD segment and take some notes. Set up DVD equipment before the session begins. If you will not be showing the DVD, summarize the "Chapter Overview" for the group.

TIP

Encourage the group to follow along in their books as you (or volunteers) read each quotation.

3. Think about a time in your life when you felt as if the whole world was conspiring against you or when you or a loved one felt captive to something or someone else—perhaps a bad habit, a pessimistic outlook, a pattern of destructive behavior, or something more difficult. How might this theory about God entering into our struggle, determined to win us back to health and life, help you during a time like that?

ACTIVITY: PRAYER FOR DELIVERANCE

Pass out sheets of lined paper and invite participants to think about an area in their lives where they feel they are struggling or feel oppressed or trapped. Remind them that they are not the first to feel this way. The book of Psalms, the songbook of ancient Israel, is filled with prayers both requesting and giving thanks for deliverance—from enemies, oppression, illness, adversity, and more. Choose one or two of the following psalms to read aloud: Psalms 3, 4, 6, 10, 69, 70, 71, 73, 120, 121, and 124. Then invite participants to write their own prayers asking God to enter into and help them get through their struggles. Encourage participants to be concrete not only in naming their struggles, but also in describing what release or deliverance would look like. If they wish, when they are done writing, participants may share or pray these prayers.

> **TIP**
>
> Read the listed psalms ahead of time and choose two or three to read, or assign the various psalms to different persons and discuss them. You may also want participants to discuss and decide ahead of time whether to share the prayers that are written, as that may shape what they decide to write.

Open Scripture (20 minutes)

JOHN 18:1-11; 19:16-30

We became familiar with John's passion in the previous chapter on the four portraits of the cross found in the Gospels. Now, having read this week's chapter on the ransom and victory theory of atonement, we will revisit two scenes from John's Gospel, the Gospel that lends itself most easily to this understanding of the cross. Read aloud the passages indicated.

Discuss:
1. What words would you use to describe Jesus, as portrayed by John?
2. How does that portrayal match or connect with your own picture or understanding of Jesus? What is similar? What is different?
3. What is comforting, helpful, or inspiring about John's portrayal? What is troubling or confusing?
4. In your life, when would this picture of Jesus have been most helpful?

SUPPLIES
- ☐ Bibles
- ☐ Session handout
- ☐ Copies of *Making Sense of the Cross*
- ☐ Lined paper and pencils and/or pens
- ☐ Paper napkins or scratch paper; gel pens or fine-line markers

> **TIP**
>
> Participants may feel hesitant about drawing at first, as many of us don't think of ourselves as particularly artistic or creative. The point isn't to hang these pictures in a gallery, but to help participants remember the key dynamics of the theory by approaching it from a different, less cognitive angle that invites our active participation. If participants need some help getting started, encourage them to look at the illustrations in *Making Sense of the Cross* or to do an online search of religious symbols.

SUPPLIES
- ☐ Chart paper from IQ Time
- ☐ Copies of *Making Sense of the Cross*
- ☐ Session handout

BONUS ACTIVITY: THE BACK OF A NAPKIN

To explain an idea to a friend or family member, we might grab a pen and draw some stick figures or a simple diagram on the back of a napkin. How would we do this for the ransom and victory theory of atonement? Distribute paper napkins or scratch paper and gel pens or fine-line markers. Invite participants to think about explaining or describing the theory with a symbol, diagram, picture, emblem, icon, or stick figures. They could, for example, sketch something with theological significance (a cross shaped like a dagger representing the battle God enters into, or Jesus pulling Adam and Eve from death); a scene from a biblical story that connects with the theory (Jesus carrying his cross himself), or an object or emblem that captures the spirit of the theory (a sword or shield). Allow a few minutes for sketching; then have volunteers share their "back of a napkin" drawings.

Extending the Conversation (10 minutes)

LOOKING BACK

Review the list made during IQ Time. Which insights and questions have been answered or clarified? Which remain unanswered? Ask participants to share additional questions or insights that have surfaced during your time together.

LOOKING AHEAD

Direct the group to the session handout and review ways to prepare for your next meeting.

1. Before reading chapter four, write down some of your thoughts about the biblical phrase "he died for our sins." What do you think that means? What images come to mind when you hear it?
2. Read chapter four in *Making Sense of the Cross*—"Substitution, Satisfaction, and Sacrifice."
3. Jot down any insights or questions you have after reading the chapter. In particular, pay attention to your reaction to the idea that God sends Jesus to pay our debt and/or be punished in our place. Does this make sense? How is it helpful or unhelpful to picture atonement in this way?

Optional: Chapter four will reference Charles Dicken's classic story, *A Tale of Two Cities*. If participants have time, they could watch a movie version of this story. Also, Mel Gibson's *The Passion of the Christ* (20th Century Fox, 2004) is a modern telling of the story of Jesus' crucifixion that operates within the substitution theory of atonement. If participants have time, they may want to view this; if they do so, they should be warned of the graphic nature of the film.

Session 3 Handout

Ransom and Victory

FOCUS STATEMENT

The theory or model of atonement that was popular for much of the first thousand years in Christian history emphasizes the titanic struggle between God and Satan for the fate of humanity, a struggle that culminates in God's triumph through the cross and resurrection of Jesus.

CONVERSATION STARTER

Discuss:
1. What do you find comforting—or uncomfortable—about the idea that the cross is too big for any one theory or model of atonement to explain? What might still be helpful about knowing and understanding several different theories of atonement?
2. When have you experienced "atonement"—that is, the healing or restoration of a relationship that was broken? How might recalling these experiences help you approach our discussions of the cross?
3. Think about a time in your life when you felt as if the whole world was conspiring against you or when you or a loved one felt captive to something or someone else—perhaps a bad habit, a pessimistic outlook, a pattern of destructive behavior, or something more difficult. How might this theory about God entering into our struggle, determined to win us back to health and life, help you during a time like that?

JOHN 18:1-11; 19:16-30

Discuss:
1. What words would you use to describe Jesus, as portrayed by John?
2. How does that portrayal match or connect with your own picture or understanding of Jesus? What is similar? What is different?
3. What is comforting, helpful, or inspiring about John's portrayal? What is troubling or confusing?
4. In your life, when would this picture of Jesus have been most helpful?

LOOKING AHEAD

1. Before reading chapter four, write down some of your thoughts about the biblical phrase "he died for our sins." What do you think that means? What images come to mind when you hear it?
2. Read chapter four in *Making Sense of the Cross*—"Substitution, Satisfaction, and Sacrifice."
3. Jot down any insights or questions you have after reading the chapter. In particular, pay attention to your reaction to the idea that God sends Jesus to pay our debt and/or be punished in our place. Does this make sense? How is it helpful or unhelpful to picture atonement in this way?

session 4
Substitution, Satisfaction, and Sacrifice

Prepare

FOCUS STATEMENT

A second theory of atonement, which has been popular for much of the last thousand years, revolves around the idea that Jesus paid for, or was punished for, the debt of honor and justice that humanity owes God because of sin.

CHAPTER OVERVIEW

The ransom and victory theory of atonement was popular for much of the first thousand years of the Christian church, particularly during the times when Christians found themselves persecuted or oppressed. Theologians eventually came to challenge a central premise of the theory: that God had to win back humanity from the devil by ransoming, paying, or tricking the devil. To one theologian in particular, Anselm of Canterbury, it seemed not just untenable but actually beneath God's honor to imagine that God would need to bargain with the devil.

In fact, the notion of God's honor is at the core of Anselm's theological work. Living in the feudal era of kings, queens, and absolute monarchy, Anselm was keenly aware of the debt of honor and obedience that all humanity owes God, creator of the cosmos and king of the universe. Human sin is therefore an offense against God's honor and even a disruption of the cosmic balance. The reality of sin therefore places both humanity and God in a bind.

For humans, the dilemma is that we can never repay God or restore the balance to the universe disrupted by our sin. Even if we lived perfectly after having sinned but once, we would only be rendering to God what God deserved. There is no way to accumulate an abundance of obedience or honor with which to make up for our sin. We are therefore doomed to fall short of God's glory and die. For God, the dilemma is that God still loves wayward humans and does not want them to perish, but cannot change the moral order of the universe. Overlooking our offenses or the moral order of the world would jeopardize God's sovereignty.

Having constructed the problem in this way, Anselm believed that Jesus is God's—and our!—answer because he is, to borrow from the doctrine of the Incarnation, the "God-man," fully God and fully human. Because Jesus is God, he lives a sinless life and satisfies God's demand for obedience and honor. More than that, Jesus dies on the cross in innocence and perfect obedience, therefore rendering God even more honor than God expects. This creates an abundance of honor. At the same time, because Jesus is human, he can represent humanity before God—that is, stand in for us—and also give to us his abundance of honor. In other words, Jesus both represents humanity as the one perfect human and gives us his additional honor to "pay back" the debt of honor humans cannot pay.

There is a tight, clear logic to Anselm's theory that made it almost immediately popular. This substitutionary theory was later expanded by two influential theologians—Thomas Aquinas and John Calvin—who shifted the emphasis from God's honor to God's justice. Seen this way, human sin is an offense against God's justice and must be punished to uphold the validity of God's law. Jesus, the God-man, stands in for humanity and is actually punished in our place, in this way "taking on our sins." Because he is God, he lives without sin and does not deserve to be punished. Because he is human, he can represent us and be punished in our place. What we deserve—punishment and death—is doled out to Jesus instead. What Jesus deserves—eternal life—is given to us so long as we recognize and believe in what Jesus has done for us.

Though immensely popular in many corners of the church, the substitutionary theory has some marked shortcomings and raises serious questions. In particular, this theory takes God's justice more seriously than it does God's love. That is, God's justice must be satisfied—someone must be punished—before God can act toward us in a loving way. Even saying that God sends Jesus out of love in the first place doesn't diminish the fact that God cannot forgive us without blood being shed. Can we really call what happens in this theory *forgiveness* if someone has to pay for it? And if Jesus is punished instead of us, can we really say that God forgives us, or does God just find someone else to punish?

> **TIP**
>
> The theory formulated by Anselm and developed by Aquinas and Calvin very much fits our own sensibilities about debits and credits. It may be helpful to think about some of the areas of your life where this kind of "accounting" language is helpful and where it is not.

BEFORE YOU BEGIN

In this chapter we consider the second of three theories of atonement. Keep in mind that as we look at these theories, we will draw out both what is helpful and what is less helpful about each one. Take a moment to remember a time when you've heard or seen Jesus described as a substitute for us or a sacrifice for our sins. (This might have been in a sermon, Bible reading, song, movie, or image.) What did you think? How did you feel? How was this helpful or unhelpful to you at the time?

SESSION INSTRUCTIONS

1. Read chapter four in *Making Sense of the Cross* and this Leader Guide session completely. Highlight or underline any portions you wish to emphasize with the group. Note also any bonus activities you want to do.
2. As always, it will help to have a whiteboard or newsprint available. If you plan to do any special activities, check to see what materials you'll need, if any.

FACILITATOR'S PRAYER

Spend some time in prayer for those who will be coming to this class, for yourself, and for the session ahead. If it is helpful, you may use this prayer as a guide:

Dear God, bless each one who comes to this study and bless me as a leader. Help us to recognize how much our sin grieves you and diminishes our enjoyment of life, that we might know and rejoice in your forgiveness. Amen.

Gather (10 minutes)

WELCOME AND CHECK-IN

Welcome the group. Take special care to recognize and welcome any new participants. Take time to ask if anyone has had an additional insight or question about the previous session and conversation that he or she would like to share.

OPENING PRAYER

Dear God, you desire only good for all of your children and are grieved when we hurt ourselves and each other through sin. Help us grow in our appreciation of just how much you love us and the lengths to which you would go to communicate that love. In Jesus' name. Amen.

INSIGHTS AND QUESTIONS (IQ) TIME

Invite participants to share any insights they had while reading chapter four. List these insights on chart paper where all can see.

Ask the group to share any questions they have about what they read. Collect these on chart paper as well.

Set the lists aside so you can return to them at the end of the session.

SUPPLIES
- [ ] Name tags
- [ ] Pens
- [ ] Snacks or a meal (optional)
- [ ] Chart paper
- [ ] Markers
- [ ] Copies of *Making Sense of the Cross*

TIP

Because this theory has some similarities with accounting, it may be helpful to have folks talk about some ways in which accounting is very helpful—setting the family budget, balancing your checkbook, paying off a mortgage—and where it is not.

Session 4
Substitution, Satisfaction, and Sacrifice

Join the Conversation (20 minutes)

VIDEO INTRODUCTION

Watch the video segment for session four. The course author will introduce the key concepts from the book and prepare the group for the activities that follow.

CONVERSATION STARTER

Read these quotations from chapter four of *Making Sense of the Cross*; then invite the participants to discuss the questions that follow.

> "Because Jesus is God's Son, Jesus is perfectly obedient. In fact, he's more than obedient. He not only lives a sinless life, but he actually goes to the cross and dies out of his devotion to God. He renders complete honor to God, and his death is even more than God would normally expect and so must be rewarded. Jesus can then share that reward with all humanity. He can render God sufficient honor that not only satisfies what God deserves, but also leaves enough left over to cover what we owe as well…. Because Jesus is also human, his payment counts as ours. That is, Jesus is able to serve as a substitute for us. Again, God can't simply pay our debt—that wouldn't be fair—but Jesus, as a human, can pay back the debt for us." (pp. 108-109)

> "I actually do like that it's logical. It all adds up—like accounting. But that's also the problem. Life isn't like accounting. I mean, some parts are—when we use our credit cards, take out a loan to buy a house, and all that. But the most important parts of life aren't about debits and credits; they're about relationships. I can't imagine running my personal life like a bank does its business….Think about it: keeping track of what everyone owes you and what you owe everyone else. Making sure that every offense, every slight, every injury is accounted for and duly punished. You'd drive yourself—and everyone around you—nuts if you tried." (p. 113)

> "Is it really forgiveness if Jesus had to pay for it? Think about it: if I loan you money, and you can't pay me back, so I find someone who can, I didn't forgive you anything. I just helped you pay it back. Maybe that's nice, but it's not forgiveness." (p. 121)

SUPPLIES
- [ ] *Making Sense of the Cross* DVD
- [ ] TV and DVD player (or computer, projection system, and screen)
- [ ] Copies of *Making Sense of the Cross*
- [ ] Session handout (p. 40)

TIP

Preview the DVD segment and take some notes. Set up DVD equipment before the session begins. If you will not be showing the DVD, summarize the "Chapter Overview" for the group.

TIP

Encourage the group to follow along in their books as you (or volunteers) read each quotation.

Discuss:
1. Does Anselm's explanation of why Jesus had to die on the cross make sense to you? What do you understand and/or like about it? What seems confusing or troubling?
2. Are there times that you do, in fact, have to keep track of favors, insults, etc. in a relationship? When? And when it is not helpful to do so?
3. When have you felt like you were in someone's debt? What was that like? When have you felt truly and fully forgiven? What did that feel like?

ACTIVITY: COST ACCOUNTING

Tell participants that they will be taking stock of what's happened in the last seven days. Have each participant make two columns on a piece of scratch paper. In one column, participants will write down everything they did wrong and everything they think others did wrong to them. In the other column, they will write down everything they did right and everything others did for them that was helpful. After a few moments, discuss what it feels like to keep track of all the details of our lives in this way. In particular, ask how participants feel about those who showed up on their lists and how this activity made them feel about themselves. Can they imagine keeping track of their own and everyone else's offenses? What would that do to relationships? Further, is "keeping track" how they believe God is most active in their lives and the world? If not, what *do* they think God is most concerned about?

> **TIP**
>
> It may be odd, unusual, or even difficult for people to try to write down all the bad things that have happened to them (or that they've done to others) in the last week. That's okay, as that discomfort is part of the exercise. When it happens, ask participants to talk about how they feel and why.

Open Scripture (20 minutes)

2 CORINTHIANS 5:17-20

This passage is at the heart of the Apostle Paul's theology and is worth reading aloud slowly, perhaps more than once.

Discuss:
1. What stands out to you as you hear Paul's language? What makes an impression? What seems most clear or most confusing?
2. To be "reconciled" to someone is to get over your anger toward that person, to relinquish your claim or hold on that one. In Anselm's theory, who needs to be reconciled to whom? That is, who is angry and needs to be satisfied?
3. Based on this Scripture text, who needs to be reconciled to whom? Who is angry and needs to get beyond that? In light of Paul's theology, what does it mean to you to be "a new creation"?

SUPPLIES
- [ ] Bibles
- [ ] Session handout
- [ ] Copies of *Making Sense of the Cross*
- [ ] Lined paper and pencils and/or pens
- [ ] Paper napkins or scratch paper; gel pens or fine-line markers

BONUS ACTIVITY: THE BACK OF A NAPKIN

For this session, do the "back of a napkin" activity with the substitutionary theory of atonement. Distribute paper napkins or scratch paper and gel pens or fine-line markers. Invite participants to think about explaining or describing the theory with a symbol, diagram, picture, emblem, icon, or stick figures. They could, for example, sketch something with theological significance (a pair of scales weighing our sins on one side and Jesus' merit on the other, or Jesus standing before a judge's bench), a scene from a biblical story that connects with the theory (Jesus dying in great agony), or an object or emblem that captures the spirit of the theory (a balance sheet). Allow a few minutes for sketching; then have volunteers share their "back of a napkin" drawings.

Extending the Conversation (10 minutes)

LOOKING BACK

Review the lists made during IQ Time. Which insights and questions have been answered or clarified? Which remain unanswered? Ask participants to share additional questions or insights that have surfaced during your time together.

LOOKING AHEAD

Direct the group to the session handout and review ways to prepare for your next meeting.

1. Before reading chapter five, write down some of your thoughts about the biblical phrase, "God is love." What do you think that means? What images come to mind when you hear it?
2. Read chapter five in *Making Sense of the Cross*—"Example and Encouragement."
3. Jot down any insights or questions you have after reading the chapter. In particular, pay attention to your reaction to the idea that God sends Jesus to be an example of perfect love, as well as to inspire us to love others. Does this make sense? What is helpful or unhelpful in picturing atonement in this way?

Optional: The 1989 film *Jesus of Montreal* (Koch Lorber Films) follows a cast of actors who decide to put on a passion play. As their work goes on, their lives resemble more and more the lives of the characters they play. If you have time, you may want to watch this film together or independently and think about the power of Jesus as an example.

TIP

Participants may feel hesitant about drawing at first, as many of us don't think of ourselves as particularly artistic or creative. The point isn't to hang these pictures in a gallery, but to help participants remember the key dynamics of the theory by approaching it from a different, less cognitive angle that invites our active participation. If participants need some help getting started, encourage them to look at the illustrations in *Making Sense of the Cross* or to do an online search of religious symbols.

SUPPLIES
- ☐ Chart paper from IQ Time
- ☐ Copies of *Making Sense of the Cross*
- ☐ Session handout

TIP

You may wish to keep the IQ lists and review them as you prepare for the next session.

Session 4 Handout

Substitution, Satisfaction, and Sacrifice

FOCUS STATEMENT

A second theory of atonement, which has been popular for much of the last thousand years, revolves around the idea that Jesus paid for, or was punished for, the debt of honor and justice that humanity owes God because of sin.

CONVERSATION STARTER

Discuss:
1. Does Anselm's explanation of why Jesus had to die on the cross make sense to you? What do you understand and/or like about it? What seems confusing or troubling?
2. Are there times that you do, in fact, have to keep track of favors, insults, etc. in a relationship? When? And when it is not helpful to do so?
3. When have you felt like you were in someone's debt? What was that like? When have you felt truly and fully forgiven? What did that feel like?

2 CORINTHIANS 5:17-20

Discuss:
1. What stands out to you as you hear Paul's language? What makes an impression? What seems most clear or most confusing?
2. To be "reconciled" to someone is to get over your anger toward that person, to relinquish your claim or hold on that one. In Anselm's theory, who needs to be reconciled to whom? That is, who is angry and needs to be satisfied?
3. Based on this Scripture text, who needs to be reconciled to whom? Who is angry and needs to get beyond that? In light of Paul's theology, what does it mean to you to be "a new creation"?

LOOKING AHEAD

1. Before reading chapter five, write down some of your thoughts about the biblical phrase, "God is love." What do you think that means? What images come to mind when you hear it?
2. Read chapter five in *Making Sense of the Cross*—"Example and Encouragement."
3. Jot down any insights or questions you have after reading the chapter. In particular, pay attention to your reaction to the idea that God sends Jesus to be an example of perfect love, as well as to inspire us to love others. Does this make sense? What is helpful or unhelpful in picturing atonement in this way?

session 5
Example and Encouragement

Prepare

FOCUS STATEMENT

The third theory of atonement we will examine together strongly rejects any notion of God needing a blood sacrifice in order to forgive sin and instead emphasizes the cross as a powerful example of God's great love for us, an example that both teaches and inspires us to love others.

CHAPTER OVERVIEW

As popular as the substitutionary theory of atonement has been, particularly in Roman Catholic and, later, conservative Protestant circles, it had its critics from the beginning. Chief among them was Peter Abelard, a younger contemporary of Anselm of Canterbury, who leveled several critiques. First, and as we noticed, the substitutionary theory seems to underplay God's love severely. Second, this theory makes no demand for, and provides no means for, changing the hearts of believers. That is, believers may be forgiven for Jesus' sake, but they are no different. Third, Abelard questioned how the enormous sin of putting Jesus, the Son of God, to death could possibly make up for the much smaller sin, in comparison, of Adam and Eve eating the forbidden fruit.

In place of a theory that focuses on God's justice and righteous demand for punishment, Abelard proposes an understanding of the cross that is anchored in God's great love for the world and God's desire that we love each other. The cross, then, is not the place where we see God's wrath at human sin poured out onto Jesus, but instead is the place where we see God's love for us and all people poured out. Out of love, God sent Jesus to proclaim a kingdom of love, the kingdom of God, and to demonstrate the character of that love through his preaching, teaching, healing, miracles, and ministry of compassion. Again and again Jesus announced God's forgiveness and mercy in both word and deed. And, when this threatened the powers that be, Jesus went to the cross rather than sacrifice his commitment to God's love, showing us in this way just how much God loves us.

How does this achieve at-one-ment? According to Abelard, the great problem for humanity is that we are separated from God primarily by our inability to love as God loves. Jesus thereby furnishes an example for us. That is, Jesus shows us how to love each other. By paying attention to how Jesus interacted with others and by listening to his teaching, we learn what it is to love. But Jesus also shows us just how much God loves us, enough to go to the

> **TIP**
>
> Although this theory of atonement is not as well known in the popular religious culture as the substitutionary theory, people may find themselves resonating to the simple and clear emphasis on God's love. It may help to allow people to talk about what they appreciate about this theory. Does it help them think and talk about God in ways that seem more natural to them?

cross out of love. This second element of Jesus' life and death was the crucial element for Abelard, who believed that it is only when we are caught up in the depth of God's love for us that we are transformed and can then turn and love others by following Jesus' example.

Later followers of Abelard also stressed that Jesus created a community of followers, first in his disciples and later in the church. This community embodies the love of God and represents the kingdom of God Jesus proclaimed on earth. Encouraging each other to follow Jesus, we become—as the Apostle Paul described—the body of Christ, living together in mutual love.

Abelard's theory of atonement stands as a marked alternative to the one first articulated by Anselm. It clearly shifts the emphasis from God's justice to God's love. For this reason it has attracted followers, not only in Abelard's day, but increasingly in our own. Despite its clear strengths—focusing on God's love; taking all of Jesus' life seriously, not just his cross; and giving important counsel on the shape of our Christian life today—it also has limitations. In particular, critics have wondered why, on the whole, Christians don't seem to be transformed by God's love. That is, while there are many good Christians who love and care for each other, there are many who do not. Christians have done both great good and great harm. Further, they don't seem to have a corner on the market of goodness, as many persons of other faiths have followed Jesus' example as well or better than his professed followers.

At the heart of all these critiques is the concern that if atonement is achieved by our transformation into more loving and lovable creatures through the power of Christ's example and encouragement, then it doesn't seem to have worked very well. Some have asked whether there has been any meaningful atonement to talk about.

BEFORE YOU BEGIN

Think about some of the most important and positive relationships in your own life and how the love that has characterized those relationships continues to shape you. Similarly, consider times when you have made real changes in your life and the support you received that made it possible for lasting change to occur.

SESSION INSTRUCTIONS

1. Read chapter five in *Making Sense of the Cross* and this Leader Guide session completely. Highlight or underline any portions you wish to emphasize with the group. Note also any bonus activities you want to do.
2. As always, it will help to have a whiteboard or newsprint available. If you plan to do any special activities, check to see what materials you'll need, if any.

Session 5
Example and Encouragement

FACILITATOR'S PRAYER

Spend some time in prayer for those who will be coming to this class, for yourself, and for the session ahead. If it is helpful, you may use this prayer as a guide:

Dear God, bless each one who comes to this study, and bless me as a leader. Bless our time and study together so that we may understand just how much you love us. Amen.

Gather (10 minutes)

WELCOME AND CHECK-IN

Welcome the group. Take special care to recognize and welcome any new participants. Take time to ask if anyone has had an additional insight or question about the previous session and conversation that he or she would like to share.

OPENING PRAYER

Dear God, we hear in Scripture that you love the world so much that you are willing to give anything, even your own Son, so that we might know your love and in this way find life. Help us to hear and believe this word and promise, and help us through our conversation and study to love others as you have loved us. In Jesus' name. Amen.

INSIGHTS AND QUESTIONS (IQ) TIME

Invite participants to share any insights they had while reading chapter five. List these insights on chart paper where all can see.

Ask the group to share any questions they have about what they read. Collect these on chart paper as well.

Set the lists aside so you can return to them at the end of the session.

SUPPLIES
- ☐ Name tags
- ☐ Pens
- ☐ Snacks or a meal (optional)
- ☐ Chart paper
- ☐ Markers
- ☐ Copies of *Making Sense of the Cross*

Join the Conversation (20 minutes)

SUPPLIES
- ☐ *Making Sense of the Cross* DVD
- ☐ TV and DVD player (or computer, projection system, and screen)
- ☐ Copies of *Making Sense of the Cross*
- ☐ Session handout (p. 47)

TIP

Preview the DVD segment and take some notes. Set up DVD equipment before the session begins. If you will not be showing the DVD, summarize the "Chapter Overview" for the group.

TIP

Encourage the group to follow along in their books as you (or volunteers) read each quotation.

VIDEO INTRODUCTION

Watch the video segment for session five. The course author will introduce the key concepts from the book and prepare the group for the activities that follow.

CONVERSATION STARTER

Read these quotations from chapter five of *Making Sense of the Cross*; then invite the participants to discuss the questions that follow.

> "God not only sends Jesus out of love, but Jesus also teaches us again and again about just how much God loves us. Think of his parable of the prodigal son. In the story, the younger son (the prodigal son) runs off and wastes his inheritance. But when he returns home a mess, his father embraces him and throws him a party. He still loves his son. Jesus teaches us that God is, first and foremost, not just about love in general but is actually in love with all of us." (pp. 132-133)

> "For Abelard and those who follow him, there isn't quite the same sense of brokenness, of hopelessness, that colors the other theories. In the ransom theory, things are hopeless because we've become captive to the devil and there's absolutely nothing we can do to escape that. In the substitution theory, it's hopeless because we owe God complete obedience and honor, but we've totally wrecked that through our sin and so deserve punishment, and, again, there's absolutely no way we can escape that condition. With Abelard, though, the problem is that because God is perfect love and we often fail to love others, we can't live with God eternally. However, if we learn to love and are inspired to love, then we *can* live with God." (p. 136)

> "Don't get me wrong. It's not that I don't think love is the ticket; I also agree that Christians should model a new kind of community, one that's based on love. But, to be perfectly honest, it's not what I see. I mean, I know there are some great congregations and some really great people at church. But let's face it, Christians have done a lot of harm throughout history, too. Just think of the Crusades, or the Inquisition, or the Christians who opposed civil rights, or some of the hateful rhetoric you hear today." (p. 142)

Discuss:
1. Each theory of atonement stems from a particular picture of God. What picture of God is assumed in Abelard's theory? What kinds of words come to mind when you think of the God Abelard imagines?
2. Abelard's theory of atonement has a more optimistic view of humanity—that is, he believes we are capable of change, even

transformation. In what ways is this view encouraging or helpful? Does it have limitations, and if so, what are they?
3. Think of a time when you—or someone you knew—felt so caught up in a sense of love that it was easy to love others. What was that like? Also think of a time when it felt very difficult, or even impossible, to love others as you knew God wanted you to. What was that like, and what made it so difficult?

ACTIVITY: POINTS OF VIEW

Sometimes looking at a parable through the eyes of different characters can help us enter more fully into the story and feel its impact. Two of the most well-known and powerful parables in the Bible are from the Gospel of Luke: the parable of the good Samaritan (Luke 10:25-37) and the parable of the prodigal son (Luke 15:11-32). Each parable has some significant characters. In the good Samaritan, there are four: the man who is beaten, the priest, the Levite, and the Samaritan. (If you need a fifth character, you could include the keeper of the inn where the Samaritan leaves the beaten man.) In the prodigal son parable, there are three characters: the younger son, father, and older brother. Have participants form groups of three or four (or five if that works better) and assign one of the parables to each group. Instruct groups to read the assigned parable aloud once or twice, assign characters to group members, and have each character tell the story from their point of view, explaining their role, motives, and outcomes. (So, for instance, the priest might explain all the things he had to do at the Temple and why it was just impossible to help that day, although he did pray for the man who was beaten. Or the beaten man might talk about what it was like to be passed over twice and then be helped by a detested foreigner.) After the groups have done this, invite them to rejoin the large group to discuss what each parable teaches about love. Why is love important? Why is it so hard at times?

> **TIP**
>
> Some participants will "warm up" to this exercise more quickly than others. You can help groups move forward by encouraging people who find it easier to get into character to go first.

Open Scripture (20 minutes)

JOHN 3:16-21; ROMANS 5:1-11; 1 CORINTHIANS 13; 1 JOHN 4:7-12

Each of these passages deals with love: God's love for us and the world and/or the kind of love we have for each other. You can take them in turns, assign individuals distinct passages, or divide participants into several "study groups" to consider a passage together.

Discuss:
1. How do we know that God loves us?
2. What do these passages tell us about the character of Christian love?
3. How does knowing that God loves us make it possible for us to love others?

SUPPLIES
- ☐ Bibles
- ☐ Session handout
- ☐ Copies of *Making Sense of the Cross*
- ☐ Lined paper and pencils and/or pens
- ☐ Paper napkins or scratch paper; gel pens or fine-line markers

> **TIP**
>
> Participants may feel hesitant about drawing at first, as many of us don't think of ourselves as particularly artistic or creative. The point isn't to hang these pictures in a gallery, but to help participants remember the key dynamics of the theory by approaching it from a different, less cognitive angle that invites our active participation. If participants need some help getting started, encourage them to look at the illustrations in *Making Sense of the Cross* or to do an online search of religious symbols.

SUPPLIES
- ☐ Chart paper from IQ Time
- ☐ Copies of *Making Sense of the Cross*
- ☐ Session handout

> **TIP**
>
> You may wish to keep the IQ lists and review them as you prepare for the next session.

BONUS ACTIVITY: THE BACK OF A NAPKIN

For this session, do the "back of a napkin" activity with the example and encouragement theory of atonement. Distribute paper napkins or scratch paper and gel pens or fine-line markers. Invite participants to think about explaining or describing the theory with a symbol, diagram, picture, emblem, icon, or stick figures. They could, for example, sketch something with theological significance (a cross over the globe to represent God's love for all the world), a scene from a biblical story that connects with the theory (the good Samaritan carrying the beaten man), or an object or emblem that captures the spirit of the theory (a heart). Allow a few minutes for sketching; then have volunteers share their "back of a napkin" drawings.

Extending the Conversation (10 minutes)

LOOKING BACK

Review the lists made during IQ Time. Which insights and questions have been answered or clarified? Which remain unanswered? Ask participants to share additional questions or insights that have surfaced during your time together.

LOOKING AHEAD

Direct the group to the session handout and review ways to prepare for your next meeting.

1. Before reading chapter six, write down some of your thoughts about the difference between experience and theory. What kinds of things can you learn in theory? What kinds of things will you never really know until you experience them firsthand?
2. Read chapter six in *Making Sense of the Cross*—"Event and Experience."
3. Jot down any insights or questions you have after reading the chapter. In particular, pay attention to your reaction to the idea that the Bible seeks not only to tell us *about* the cross but also to create for us an experience *of* the cross. Does this make sense? What other situations in life are like this?
4. Encourage people to bring their collages from session one to the next session.

Optional: Several films offer insight into how the sacrifice of another can shape our lives profoundly. Two good examples are *Gallipoli* (Paramount Pictures, 1981) and *The Spitfire Grill* (Turner Home Entertainment, 1996). Either or both would serve as good preparation for reading chapter six.

Session 5 Handout

Example and Encouragement

FOCUS STATEMENT

The third theory of atonement we will examine together strongly rejects any notion of God needing a blood sacrifice in order to forgive sin and instead emphasizes the cross as a powerful example of God's great love for us, an example that both teaches and inspires us to love others.

CONVERSATION STARTER

Discuss:
1. Each theory of atonement stems from a particular picture of God. What picture of God is assumed in Abelard's theory? What kinds of words come to mind when you think of the God Abelard imagines?
2. Abelard's theory of atonement has a more optimistic view of humanity—that is, he believes we are capable of change, even transformation. In what ways is this view encouraging or helpful? Does it have limitations, and if so, what are they?
3. Think of a time when you—or someone you knew—felt so caught up in a sense of love that it was easy to love others. What was that like? Also think of a time when it felt very difficult, or even impossible, to love others as you knew God wanted you to. What was that like, and what made it so difficult?

JOHN 3:16-21; ROMANS 5:1-11; 1 CORINTHIANS 13; 1 JOHN 4:7-12

Discuss:
1. How do we know that God loves us?
2. What do these passages tell us about the character of Christian love?
3. How does knowing that God loves us make it possible for us to love others?

LOOKING AHEAD

1. Before reading chapter six, write down some of your thoughts about the difference between experience and theory. What kinds of things can you learn in theory? What kinds of things will you never really know until you experience them firsthand?
2. Read chapter six in *Making Sense of the Cross*—"Event and Experience."
3. Jot down any insights or questions you have after reading the chapter. In particular, pay attention to your reaction to the idea that the Bible seeks not only to tell us *about* the cross but also to create for us an experience *of* the cross. Does this make sense? What other situations in life are like this?
4. If possible, bring your collage from session one to the next session.

session 6
Event and Experience

Prepare

FOCUS STATEMENT

Atonement, like the cross and resurrection, isn't an idea that we can comprehend and master, but an experience of the grace of God that leads us through death to new life.

CHAPTER OVERVIEW

We began our investigation of the cross by taking seriously the Christian affirmation that it is in the cross and resurrection of Jesus that God is revealed to us most fully and truly. That is, whatever we may think about God, we must put those thoughts and speculations to the test in light of what God actually did in the cross, and even be willing to call into question our assumptions about God's power and might, for instance, in light of the vulnerability we see displayed in the cross.

For this reason, we turned next to look at the four Gospel accounts of Jesus' cross, noticing both the broad similarity in terms of the outline or general plot of the story they tell, as well as the manifold and distinct differences in each account. We soon realized that these differences become very important clues to hearing each author's distinct confession of faith about the meaning and significance of Jesus' death and resurrection. While each Gospel, therefore, gives a somewhat different confession, we only appreciate the fullness of what God has accomplished— and is still accomplishing!— through the cross by holding all four confessions together. That is, we gain an appreciation for the truth of and about Jesus as we look at it from the four vantage points, or perspectives, offered by the four Gospels.

Many Christians have also looked to the four distinct but complementary Gospels to address questions about the meaning and effect of the cross. We looked at three of these approaches to find out how each one understands the cross as the means by which God achieves atonement, the restoration and repair of our damaged relationships with God and each other. Each theory of atonement, we discovered, tends to focus on certain sections of Scripture and has its own distinct strengths as well as limitations. And so we are left to wonder, does any theory of atonement offer a comprehensive and satisfactory explanation of the cross?

But perhaps that's the wrong question. That is, perhaps the cross isn't something you can finally understand as some kind of intellectual exercise. Rather, perhaps Jesus' cross and resurrection should be understood more like the evangelists understand them—as events, things you can certainly think about, but finally must experience to really understand.

In light of this insight, the question becomes not what do the cross and resurrection *mean*, but what do they *set in motion* and *cause to happen*? For this reason, I suggest focusing on what actually happens in the biblical stories of Jesus. Notice, in particular, that when Jesus comes he proclaims the kingdom of God, a kingdom that is established by God's mercy, love, and forgiveness. But many characters—especially those who believe they can achieve righteousness on their own, and most of us, to be honest—don't really want forgiveness, because it is a reminder that we're actually sinful and in need. So Jesus is eventually put to death because he has dared to tell the truth about the sin of those around him. But he comes back because God's love is more powerful than death, and he again proclaims forgiveness, a message that points unavoidably to the human predicament of sin and simultaneously offers hope that God's love for us is stronger than our sin.

Jesus' cross and resurrection, then, tell us two truths. The first is that we are sinful, confused, hurting, and broken and cannot save ourselves. The second is that God loves us just as we are and will keep coming to us in mercy, love, and forgiveness. The first truth puts to death all of our desires to make it on our own; the second raises us to new life by promising that God will always be with us and for us . . . no matter what.

This, then, is "doing atonement"—not just talking about it as one more theory we can agree to or dismiss, but rather an actual event and experience as we are drawn into relationship with the living God. This encounter and experience puts to death all of our attempts to be in control, to go it alone, to define our lives and the world on our own terms. Simultaneously, it raises us to new life in relationship with the living and loving God. Having experienced Jesus' cross and resurrection in this way, we are joined to all other Christians to form a community of atonement—a community, that is, of forgiven sinners who, trusting in God's mercy and grace, seek to extend God's reconciling and life-giving love to all people and, indeed, all the world.

BEFORE YOU BEGIN

The primary goal of this session is to move from academic or theological analyses of the cross and resurrection to a place where participants actually experience Jesus' cross and resurrection as the death of our desire to make it on our own and the new life of being held in and by God's mercy and love. Think about a time when you felt "at one" with God and other Christians. How would you describe this? Consider sharing this experience with participants and inviting them to share similar stories.

> **TIP**
>
> This is important—but at times complex—material. It might be helpful to review sections of the book, Leader Guide, or DVD more than once. And don't feel that you have to understand everything perfectly to lead this session. As with all the central elements of our faith in God, there is an irreducible element of mystery present here. What is more important than understanding everything is simply sensing and experiencing God's profound love for us, a love that is expressed in both Jesus' cross and resurrection.

> **TIP**
>
> You and your group might want to mark the end of this study by sharing a meal together, agreeing to pray for each other in the weeks ahead, or in some other way.

SESSION INSTRUCTIONS

1. Read chapter six in *Making Sense of the Cross* and this Leader Guide session completely. Highlight or underline any portions you wish to emphasize with the group. Note also any bonus activities you want to do.
2. As always, it will help to have a whiteboard or newsprint available. If you plan to do any special activities, check to see what materials you'll need, if any.

FACILITATOR'S PRAYER

Spend some time in prayer for those who will be coming to this class, for yourself, and for the session ahead. If it is helpful, you may use this prayer as a guide:

Dear God, bless each one who comes to this study, and bless me as a leader. Help us to hear, see, feel, and experience your profound love for us as we consider the death and resurrection of your Son, Jesus. Amen.

SUPPLIES
- [ ] Name tags
- [ ] Pens
- [ ] Snacks or a meal (optional)
- [ ] Chart paper
- [ ] Markers
- [ ] Copies of *Making Sense of the Cross*

TIP

Once again, it may be helpful to remind group members that all questions and insights are welcome. There are no "wrong" questions or insights. And, if you go around the room to give everyone a chance to participate, make sure people know it's all right to "pass" or not offer an insight or question.

Gather (10 minutes)

WELCOME AND CHECK-IN

Welcome the group. Take special care to recognize and welcome any new participants. Take time to ask if anyone has had an additional insight or question about the previous session and conversation that he or she would like to share.

OPENING PRAYER

Dear God, the death and resurrection of your Son are too real, too painful, too awesome, and just too big for us to ever fully understand. And so we ask that you would not only help us think about Jesus' cross and resurrection, but also and even more to experience them as indicators of your great love for us so that we might be drawn together with all other Christians into a community of atonement and reconciliation. Amen.

INSIGHTS AND QUESTIONS (IQ) TIME

Invite participants to share any insights they had while reading chapter six. List these insights on chart paper where all can see.

Ask the group to share any questions they have about what they read. Collect these on chart paper as well.

Set the lists aside so you can return to them at the end of the session.

Session 6
Event and Experience

Join the Conversation (20 minutes)

VIDEO INTRODUCTION

Watch the video segment for session six. The course author will introduce the key concepts from the book and prepare the group for the activities that follow.

CONVERSATION STARTER

Read these quotations from chapter six of *Making Sense of the Cross*; then invite the participants to discuss the questions that follow.

> "Each of these *theories* about us and God and atonement and all are useful. But we don't live theoretically; we actually live. We aren't in a theoretical relationship with God; we're in an actual relationship. We aren't broken in theory; we're actually broken. We don't need to be fixed or healed or redeemed—or however you want to describe it—in theory; we need to be actually healed and restored. I think the problem with theories—and models, too, for that matter—is that we can look at them, discuss them, and evaluate them, but all the while never really be touched by them." (p. 151)

> "Well, most of the stuff we do in life we do because we feel like we have a good reason, even the things we do that hurt others. Obviously there are accidents, and we don't mind apologizing for those. But if a little kid takes his sister's toy, even if he knows it's wrong, he still kind of believes he deserves it and so should have it. So even though he knows he's wrong, when he's caught it still feels bad. And judging from the newspapers and my own experience, I don't think we're all that different from kids. We do things for a reason, even harmful things. The reasons might not make sense to others, but they do to us. So we don't want to get caught. And even when we know something we've done is wrong, it's still really painful to be caught, to be judged, because all of a sudden it feels like we've been found unworthy, or suddenly we're not in control anymore." (pp. 160-161)

> "We live in a world where only some people are fed, and so Jesus feeds the hungry. We live in a world where people are sick and die needlessly, and so Jesus heals them. We live in a world where strength is honored over compassion, where wealth is the measure of importance rather than integrity, where power is measured by what you can destroy rather than what you can create, and so every act of grace, every sign or miracle of compassion, every act of healing, every time Jesus embraces someone the system has declared an outcast, he is calling the whole system into question." (p. 176)

SUPPLIES
- [ ] *Making Sense of the Cross* DVD
- [ ] TV and DVD player (or computer, projection system, and screen)
- [ ] Copies of *Making Sense of the Cross*
- [ ] Session handout (p. 55)

TIP

Preview the DVD segment and take some notes. Set up DVD equipment before the session begins. If you will not be showing the DVD, summarize the "Chapter Overview" for the group.

TIP

Encourage the group to follow along in their books as you (or volunteers) read each quotation.

Discuss:
1. What's the difference between a theory about something—parenting, dating, writing, working at a particular job—and actually doing it? How does that distinction between theory and experience translate into our relationship with God? What's the difference between a theoretical faith and an experiential one?
2. Think back to a time when you were "caught" doing something you shouldn't have done. Maybe it was something big, or maybe something little. What did it feel like? How did you feel about the person who caught you? Looking back, what did it cost you? And what did it offer you? That is, did it make anything new possible?
3. We tend to think about our faith in fairly personal, even somewhat individualistic, ways. But the Bible confesses that God loves the whole world (John 3:16). How does the cross have significance for the whole world? And what about the resurrection? What does the author mean in saying that Jesus' cross calls into question "the whole system" and that the resurrection makes a promise of redemption to the whole world?

ACTIVITY: ATONEMENT ASSOCIATION

Invite participants into a process of free association, saying whatever first comes to mind when they hear a particular word. Here are some words you may want to have them free associate with: *grace, judgment, atonement, cross, love, ransom, substitution, example, experience, resurrection, Jesus, church, God.* (You can also add others.) After this time of free association, have participants discuss whether they detected any patterns in their responses. What themes, if any, kept coming up? What picture of God would someone paint after listening to their responses? If there is time, each person may want to share one key insight or question he or she now has as a result of this exercise or the conversation and study throughout this course.

> **TIP**
>
> Capturing some of the key insights and questions on chart paper may be helpful.

Session 6
Event and Experience

Open Scripture (20 minutes)

1 CORINTHIANS 1:18—2:2

This passage is considered one of the central places where the Apostle Paul expresses his "theology of the cross" as he describes how unexpected, even startling, the cross was. We read it during our first week together. Let's read and discuss it again in light of our time of study and conversation over the last six sessions.

Discuss:
1. How do you now understand Paul when he says that the message of the cross is "foolishness" and a "stumbling block"? How does the cross "trip us up"?
2. The cross, as an instrument of torture, humiliation, and execution, was about the last way anyone would have expected God to work for the salvation of the world. What does this "foolish" choice tell us about God? What does it tell us about us?
3. When have you experienced the foolishness of the cross bringing you down and the righteousness of God bringing you back up again? What was that like? How might you share that with others?

BONUS ACTIVITY: WHEN I THINK OF GOD

This is the same exercise as in the first session. Have available scissors, glue sticks, small sheets of cardstock or construction paper, and a variety of old magazines. Invite each person to page through the magazines and cut out pictures that help them imagine what the God we know best through Jesus' cross and resurrection is like; then glue the images onto cardstock or construction paper to create a collage. When these collages are complete, give participants a few moments to think about how the collage they just created compares to the one they created in the first session.

Next, invite participants to show their collages to the group and share what the various images mean to them. (If the earlier collages are available, they can be shown to the group at the same time.) Encourage participants to talk about what they have learned, insights they have gained, and questions they are asking now.

SUPPLIES
- [ ] Bibles
- [ ] Session handout
- [ ] Copies of *Making Sense of the Cross*
- [ ] Scissors
- [ ] Glue sticks
- [ ] Small sheets of cardstock or construction paper
- [ ] Old magazines
- [ ] Collages created during the first session

TIP

Participants may notice all kinds of things as they compare their two collages. Accept whatever they share about this and what they have learned since the first session, and affirm them in their growth. When it is your time to share, mentioning how much you have learned through your conversations with members of this study group may be helpful.

Extending the Conversation (10 minutes)

SUPPLIES
- ☐ Chart paper from IQ Time
- ☐ Paper and pencils or pens to capture ideas from the brainstorming

LOOKING BACK

Review the lists made during IQ Time. Which insights and questions have been answered or clarified? Which remain unanswered? Ask participants to share additional questions or insights that have surfaced during your time together.

LOOKING AHEAD

Invite participants to form groups of two or three. Give the groups five to ten minutes to brainstorm responses to these questions:

1. If we take seriously the cross, the resurrection, and atonement as actual events and experiences, how might that shape our lives? How might it shape the life of our congregation?
2. In what ways is our congregation a community of atonement? How might members and guests experience this more fully and powerfully?

After this brainstorming time, have each group report back. Collect these ideas to share with the pastor(s) and the church council or governing board of the congregation.

Session 6 Handout

Event and Experience

FOCUS STATEMENT

Atonement, like the cross and resurrection, isn't an idea that we can comprehend and master, but an experience of the grace of God that leads us through death to new life.

CONVERSATION STARTER

Discuss:
1. What's the difference between a theory about something—parenting, dating, writing, working at a particular job—and actually doing it? How does that distinction between theory and experience translate into our relationship with God? What's the difference between a theoretical faith and an experiential one?
2. Think back to a time when you were "caught" doing something you shouldn't have done. Maybe it was something big, or maybe something little. What did it feel like? How did you feel about the person who caught you? Looking back, what did it cost you? And what did it offer you? That is, did it make anything new possible?
3. We tend to think about our faith in fairly personal, even somewhat individualistic, ways. But the Bible confesses that God loves the whole world (John 3:16). How does the cross have significance for the whole world? And what about the resurrection? What does the author mean in saying that Jesus' cross calls into question "the whole system" and that the resurrection makes a promise of redemption to the whole world?

1 CORINTHIANS 1:18—2:2

Discuss:
1. How do you now understand Paul when he says that the message of the cross is "foolishness" and a "stumbling block"? How does the cross "trip us up"?
2. The cross, as an instrument of torture, humiliation, and execution, was about the last way anyone would have expected God to work for the salvation of the world. What does this "foolish" choice tell us about God? What does it tell us about us?
3. When have you experienced the foolishness of the cross bringing you down and the righteousness of God bringing you back up again? What was that like? How might you share that with others?

LOOKING AHEAD

Discuss:
1. If we take seriously the cross, the resurrection, and atonement as actual events and experiences, how might that shape our lives? How might it shape the life of our congregation?
2. In what ways is our congregation a community of atonement? How might members and guests experience this more fully and powerfully?

Session 6 Handout: *Making Sense of the Cross*. Permission is granted to reproduce this page for local use. Copyright © Augsburg Fortress, 2011.